HOW TO
Write & Release
YOUR FIRST SONG

SONGWRITING SECRETS FROM AN AWARD-WINNING ARTIST
CHRIS GREENWOOD

CONTENTS

Introduction   5

Chapter 1: Knowing Your Audience   15

Chapter 2: Developing A Songwriter's Mindset   27

Chapter 3: Filling The Well of Inspiration   43

Chapter 4: Understanding Song Structure   67

Chapter 5: Finding Your Unique Voice   81

Chapter 6: The 4 C's Of A Confident Songwriter   107

Chapter 7: Working With A Producer   121

Chapter 8: The Truth About Labels   143

Chapter 9: Becoming A Music Marketing Machine   155

Epilogue: It's Time To Write Your Dreams   181

Songwriting Secrets from an Award-Winning Artist

INTRODUCTION

Songs are not just pieces of music; they're the soundtrack to our lives

Play Beastie Boys Sabotage and I'm transfigured back to a skate park getting wild with my homies.

Press play on Guns Roses' *November Rain* and I'm transported back to a pre-teen party dancing with a girl while teachers scan the room and make sure hands stay above the waist.

Turn on Aerosmith's *I Don't Want to Miss a Thing* and I can remember kissing my wife for the first time.

Sing Chris Tomlin's *Good, Good Father* and I get all choked up with tears running down my face as I'm reminded of a time in church when God spoke to me in an incredibly powerful way.

Songs move people. They create visuals in our minds and stoke fires in our hearts. They lift us up, take us down, and allow our minds to soar.

HOW TO WRITE AND RELEASE YOUR FIRST SONG

The words we create as songwriters and performers have the power of life and death.

And we must choose what we will use our songs for.

I've stood on stage and watched thousands of people singing every lyric to some of my songs while tears ran down their faces.

I've received letters from fans telling me a song got them through college, stopped them from committing suicide, or even saved their marriage.

Watching and hearing how my songs impact people like this brings true gratification on a very personal level. It is exhilarating and inspiring, and I appreciate the amazing opportunity we have as songwriters to speak life with our songs while simultaneously painting the backdrop for our listeners' lives.

The songs we write have the capacity to change our lives too, and be a gift to future generations of our families.

Imagine how amazing it will feel to play your songs in years to come for your children and your grandkids.

When you pass down your songs as an inheritance to your children, you leave a powerful legacy: artistically and financially.

The truth is, songwriting is easy

It's just a case of building up your confidence and practicing – and these are skills which you'll get the chance to build on through this book. It's the songwriting business which is hard, and we're going to explore that too. I hope to give you an edge from my 20-plus years of writing songs full time and performing them across the globe in over 22 countries.

I'm completely self-taught: I learned to write songs and perform them by doing it over and over, and by rubbing shoulders with some of the greatest songwriters of the 21st century. I've written Billboard-charting radio hits and I've had my share of flops, but what I'm most proud of is how my songs have impacted lives of millions of people around the globe.

Songwriting is like writing a message; allowing you to speak in languages you don't know. Your songs open doors and cross the cultural barriers that normal speech can't. And when your songs have been recorded and made available, they preach their message – *your message* – 24/7.

There is nothing more fulfilling than sharing your songs while making a great living at the same time. There's a beautiful alchemy that occurs when you pour your heart into your music and your listeners connect with it to such a degree that their hearts are enriched too.

When you're new to the industry finding those listeners isn't always easy, but I've got your back in this area too. I have an extra resource I'd love to share with you: a free 5-day challenge designed to help you grow and monetize a fanbase with your newly-written songs. You'll find bonus video content, a worksheet, plus a ton of extra resources to help you through this book. I recommend you take a moment to access this exclusive area now; it's totally free and it's designed to enhance your reading experience.

Join us here: **https://www.10xyourfanbase.com/100kfans.**

If I could go back in time to when I was a new artist just starting out, I'd have loved to get my teeth into the 5-day challenge to witness the results I now know are possible. I can't wait to hear how it works out for you, too.

Songwriting as an outlet

I started writing songs when I was 22 after my dreams of becoming a skateboarder and moving down to California were shattered. Instead of taking my own life like my father did when he was down and out, I began to paint the pain through songwriting.

Songwriting is an incredible outlet for dealing with life's tough times. It's a way to release tension from inside your mind, get over heartbreak, deal with loss – or any other struggle you're facing.

I didn't start by seeking out any classical or college-level training, I just picked up a pad and pen and began writing songs in my mom's basement.

I would have laughed in your face back then if you told me my songs would be sung around the world, or that I'd be famous in a country like Japan.

I think God has a sense of humor; He likes to take the most unlikely people and do incredible things with them.

I'm not the most talented artist or songwriter but I've got a big heart filled with persistence and I'm committed to always keep learning. And that's what got me where I am today.

A dream worth advancing towards

The songs you'll write are not just words blowing in the wind; they have the ability to cause revolutions and revelations in the hearts of men and women.

It is my goal that this book will guide you as you tap into the well of inspiration and as you become a better songwriter. It is my hope that this book will help you write your first song and release it as an independent artist.

We're going to cover everything from writing stronger lyrics, verses, choruses, song titles, melodies and so much more – all with the ultimate objective to make your song as compelling as it can be. We'll look at methods for coming up with ideas, finding your voice, and gaining confidence as an artist. I'll give you my take on working with record labels and I'll talk you through how to market and share your music. You'll find the book is peppered with inside stories and pro-tips, all borne of my 20+ years in the industry.

Essentially, I want you to write songs that transcend time. I want your music to not just survive – *but thrive*. Some of my most popular songs were written over a decade ago and they still stand strong to this day. I want that for you. I want you to be able to write something that is timeless, while carving out your own space in people's hearts and ears with your songs.

That makes you limitless – and I believe wholeheartedly that is a dream worth advancing towards.

Where I'm coming from, and where we're headed

I released my first EP in 2001, so I've been writing and recording songs for over twenty years with fourteen commercially-released albums. I've had the Billboard-charting albums with #1 radio singles, Juno Awards, and songs featured in numerous TV and film productions, plus video games. I can say with 100% certainty the secret to a full-time career in music isn't the quantity of songs you've written, it's the quality and how well those hit songs are marketed.

Have you heard of the Pareto Principle? It's also sometimes referred to as the 80/20 principle, and it's the idea that the effects of most things in life aren't distributed evenly. For example, you might run a business where 80% of the profits come from 20% of the products you sell. Or you could work in an office where 80% of the work is completed by 20% of the people employed.

The point for us here is that I've written over 150 songs – yet the majority of my revenue comes from just ten of those songs.

The Pareto Principle allows us to focus our efforts in the areas where we get the most rewards.

That's why, in 2014, I took a step back from touring. Part of the reason was to raise a family, but it also gave me the space and time to start my company, Smart Music Business, in which I've coached thousands of artists and musicians to market and sell their music online.

I always knew that one of the drawbacks with great marketing is that it makes bad songs fail faster. That's why I created one of the most audacious songwriting systems, Song Launch, which acts as a guide to take you from writing a song, to recording it, to releasing it commercially.

You'll find a lot of the advice from Song Launch in this book. If you follow what I'm sharing and suggesting, you'll not only become a songwriter, but you'll understand exactly what it takes to craft a hit song and release it to the world on a global stage.

Are you with me? I really hope so. But if there's a part of you that's thinking it can't happen for you, or that you need particular equipment or training first – let me bust some of the doubts that might be dogging you before we head on in to the rest of the book.

"Never let the odds keep you from doing what you know in your heart you were meant to do." - **H. Jackson Brown JR.**

MYTH-BUSTING:
What A Songwriter Needs To Get Started

#1 – You need to have a professionally sound-proofed studio to record a hit song.

Not true. I've recorded songs under blankets and those songs are currently being played on Sirius XM radio.

#2 – You need to have an expensive microphone costing thousands to track great sounding vocals.

This is also a myth: I used a $399 Shure SM7B microphone to record multiple hit songs and some that received a $60,000 TV placement.

#3 – You have to live in Nashville or Los Angeles to get in the game.

This is totally false (though being surrounded by other industry professionals is helpful). I live in a small suburb outside of Toronto, Canada, but the internet allows me to reach a global audience. Meetings and writing sessions via Zoom and Skype have now become the norm.

#4 – You have to have the most expensive gear, latest software and plugins to make a great song.

There have been countless hits produced on FL Studio and Garage band. It's not the software it's the user.

Chapter 1:
KNOWING YOUR AUDIENCE

When it's your goal to write a song and release it out into the world, your first step is to decide who the song is for, and what the purpose is.

Are you writing a Christmas song for families to enjoy around an open fire while drinking a cup of hot chocolate?

Or do you want to write a summer-smash anthem for high school kids who've just graduated? Something for them to celebrate with as they crank the volume up on the car stereo?

Or your goal for your song might be for it to be played on a specific TV show. You might want it to perfectly complement a romantic scene, or a sad one.

Or perhaps you really want to write a fist-pumping adrenaline-charged song that could get played at the UFC, or on other televised sports shows.

Notice how those quick examples are short, but they each have a clear audience and purpose in mind. Knowing these key pieces of information is the bedrock of your song. I work with really talented producers and they always call me out when I'm not focused and when I don't know who I'm writing for.

Seriously, if I showed up at the studio and said, "Oh, let's just write a song," they'd flat-out refuse to go on that journey with me. They need to know who the song is for and what the purpose is – otherwise that song is going to be targeting an audience of zero.

I had a producer friend challenge me on a song I was writing about relationships. It was called *Too Late*, and he noticed it had some dark overtones. The song wasn't finished yet when he heard it, but I told him I was leaning towards having the relationship between two people end in the song. He had some key advice for me: apparently, the TV and film requests that had been coming in were for more positive songs. "Why not tweak the song so the vibe is more, *We got this*, instead of, *It's too late*," he suggested. I agreed and that slight change with the tone of the song changed everything, helping to narrow the focus and give clarity on who we were writing for.

Who are you writing your song for?

Here are some questions to help narrow it down:

Is your song for females or males?
How old is your target listener? Teen, adult, middle-aged, or older? Or is your song for kids? (Though if you're writing music for children you're probably going to want to target parents)
Is it for hipsters or surfers?
Church-goers or choir congregations?
Are you writing for heavy metal, gothic rock fans who just want to rock out?

Picture your listener: Who are they?
What do they look like?
Get specific: What are they wearing? What kind of haircut do they have?

Dig deeper

As well as getting a clearer idea of your listener, you can also dig deeper into the mood of the song. To kick-start this, think about the emotions you want to relate in your music.

What's the vibe or the feel of the song you want to write? Is it chilling, with a ton of Billie Eilish vibes, energetic like Nickel Back, happy like Pharrell Williams, dark like Eminem, fierce like Metallica, depressing like Nirvana, or is it sympathetic, joyful, angry… or something else?

You might think I'm cramping your style a little by getting you to think in this way, but honestly this type of focus really helps you to narrow down into a niche.

We're living in an age of technology right now where people can listen to whatever style of music they want with a push of a button. They can filter and filter their taste down to the point of a specific style of genre and sub-genre. It's not just rock, it's Celtic rock, or heavy rock, or Christian rock.

Where do you want your music to fit?
What's your niche?

Speaking the language

If you're writing a song aimed for teenagers but the lyrics are written with words that older people tend to say, then it's not likely you'll connect with your desired audience. You won't be using the right dialect or the right slang – and you won't be speaking their language. If your song doesn't speak the language of your desired audience, it won't reach them – and if it does, it will fall on deaf ears.

Early in my career I had an attitude of, "Hey man, my music is for everybody." Looking back now I see how naïve that was. When you try to write for everyone you end up reaching no one.

You can still write about universal themes that everyone can relate to while also keeping your specific audience in mind. If I write about skateboarding, I know in one way I'm alienating a large part of the population, but I'm also tapping into a massive market. If I write about war veterans I understand there's a specific group of people who will connect to that song, but that there are millions of others who have never been to war or had that experience. It doesn't mean there isn't a market for the song; Hollywood makes movies about war all the time and they sell millions.

The key is to just be okay with not reaching everyone, and to not fool yourself into thinking that you can.

Not everyone is going to like your music. The sooner you can come to grips with that and be okay with it, the more you'll increase your chance of having an amazing writing career.

Think of a handful of artists you like. If you look at their Instagram or other social media, you'll notice some attract a lot of comments and interaction from women while for others the majority of their likes and so on come from guys.

It can be 50/50, but for me, it's 70/30 with the majority of my audience being male – I know this from Spotify stats. I believe this comes down to the fact that the majority of my songs are anthem driven and very few are about love or relationships. When I do put out a song that's about love, relationships, or prayers I get my biggest response from women.

When I'm running Facebook Ads I can see who's buying music based on which song I'm promoting: when it's a rock pumping anthem song I see the majority of people who buy the track are male; when I'm promoting a softer song like *Pray or Every Time You Run*, the majority of my customers are female.

On the whole I attract more male fans because of the songs I write and release. If I focused on writing more songs directed to more women over the next two years, I'd see a shift in my fan base for sure.

I honestly don't care whether my listeners are male or female – as long as my songs are impacting people.

"I hope that what it comes down to at the end of the day is that people believe that I believe what I'm singing. It comes down to being believable." – John Mayer

The artist makes the track

Great songs are the foundation of any successful songwriter's career and lyrics are the building blocks. There wouldn't be a music industry without the songs. There'd be no tours, no booking agents, no publicists and no record labels. That's where you come in.

One of my friends Gerry always used to tell me, "It's not necessarily the track or the beat; it's the artist who makes the track great." And they were right. You could have a hit beat, a hit production, but if you don't rock a smashing vocal performance over that track – you're not going to do that track justice.

If a song sounds good with a rough vocal over a piano or acoustic guitar and zero fancy production, you know you have the makings of a great song. Always remember that the production is an amplifier of the lyrics and melody that are already there.

Have you ever had that experience where you hear a song and you love the beat but you can't stand the vocals on top of it? I'm a fan of some of Limp Bizkit's music and definitely enjoy his live shows. Yet I find that some of his songs are these super-sick rock tracks where his lyrics and performance arewere my least favorite part of the song.

Eminem is regarded as one of the greatest lyricists and songwriters ever, but when he put out his album *Encore* it received a lot of criticism. This album had the same dope production as his classics and the recording quality was top notch, but I remember reading a review from one fan who said, "It sounded like he wasn't even trying." The reason I remember that review is because that's how I felt about the album too: that it wasn't his best effort. In fairness, this can happen to all of us., especially when you've been in the industry for a while.

HOW TO WRITE AND RELEASE YOUR FIRST SONG

Great songs take effort. Just having a dope beat or a flawless production isn't what makes the song – it's what you write and perform over top of it that counts.

"Four basic premises of writing: clarity, brevity, simplicity and humanity." – William Zinsser

Songwriting Secrets from an Award-Winning Artist

INSIDE STORY:
The First Song I Ever Wrote

When I first started out in music, I was in a rap group but I left after a few months because I had a strong desire to make my own way in the industry. The first song I ever wrote as a solo artist was called Session – and it was all about the skateboarding sessions I had so often with my friends back then.

Skateboarding was a huge passion for me. I was so infatuated with it that I even sampled skateboarding trick sounds in the song, which I got from a VHS video.

Within a year or so I finally had about five songs I was very proud of and my goal was to release an EP. I thought for sure I would sell at least 50,000 copies of this EP and I had big dreams of it blowing up all over the world. My friend Pasi, who often filmed my friends and I skateboarding, said he'd shoot my first music video for me. Of course, we filmed it at an indoor skateboard park and had me skateboarding in the video.

I need to rewind a little: one of my favorite rappers growing up was Xzibit. In the 90s he brought out an album called At the *Speed of Life* and it included an enhanced CD which had a music video on it of his song *Paparazzi*. I always thought that was the coolest thing in the world, and I wanted that for my first EP. It took a little bit more time at the mastering facility to figure out how to get the music video burnt onto the disc, but it was worth it. For an independent artist to have an enhanced CD with his music video on it was a big deal – plus it was a selling point for fans and stores.

I called that first EP *Misled Youth*. Picking up the CDs for the first time is a moment I'll always remember: seeing them shrink- wrapped with my artwork on the sleeve and knowing my music was on them made me feel like a six-year old on Christmas morning.

But after a few live shows, even though we sold a bunch, I quickly found out how much hard work it was to sell music. Distribution, marketing, and awareness are all key factors that need to come into play if you want to sell 50,000 albums. I think we ended up selling 5000 physical copies – which is not bad – and I do believe that number would have been closer to 500 if I hadn't set the ambitious goal of 50,000. Like Grant Cardone says, "Go big or go bigger."

So many artists don't set a clear sales goal or have a plan about how to get their music out into the world, and then they get stuck with hundreds (or thousands) of CDs, USBs or download cards piled up in their garage or basement.

Having a clear picture of your end goal is essential and it's also motivating, providing you with a destination you can work towards. It can be the difference between making it and not making it.

I chose to release an EP rather than just a single because it was more cost-effective and I believed I could make a bigger impact with not just one but five awesome songs. This did require a lot of patience to put the songs together, finalize them and make the whole thing perfect before letting them out into the world.

iTunes and Spotify have really changed the landscape in terms of how quickly we can share our music. I know a lot of artists finish a song and whip it out there before they've got much in the way of feedback from friends or fellow artists. When I wrote and recorded Misled Youth, we had a lot more time to mull over the songs, and fix mixes, re-write lyrics, or even re-record the songs to make them the best we believed they could be.

As I write this book, I'm under a deadline. I have four weeks to write a new rock song demo for my producer so he can start making the music for it. If I don't set a deadline it's not going to get done.

Deadlines provide motivation, and motivation inspires action.

Chapter 2:
DEVELOPING A SONGWRITER'S MINDSET

A lot of artists have a hard drive full of rough demos and dozens of notebooks filled with lyrics and song ideas that never see the light of day.

Sometimes this is down to fear, and other times it's because they don't know what the steps are to take a song from an idea to a demo to a mixed and mastered song.

I had released one EP, two albums and written over fifty songs before I felt like a real songwriter. I don't know why, but it took me a long time to get confident as a songwriter, especially when it came to writing choruses.

This was partly to do with my mindset at the time, but it was also down to a lack of practice.

Two key skills: Practice and patience

When I first started out, I was heavily influenced by what I liked listening to: rap. Rappers always focus on what's called a hot sixteen bar verse. Lyrics and flow are everything, especially punch lines, which conclude with a strong statement. Because this was the genre and style I gravitated towards, I built up a lot of confidence in myself as a rapper who could write lyrics for verses – but when it came to the choruses, I felt inadequate.

I would always ask friends, family and whoever would listen to critique my songs, assuming they weren't good enough. As a rookie songwriter who was hungry to get better I opened myself up to constant criticism so I could hone my craft.

I just needed practice – and patience. Look at someone like Dolly Parton with over 3000 songs to her name and more than 20 number-one country singles – and that doesn't even include the songs she started but didn't finish.

I used to think that my first song had to be my best song and it had to be a massive hit and have an awesome music video as well as a lyric video, and I'd daydream and paint all these beautiful scenes of grandeur and hitting it big.

Now, I'm not here to tell you not to dream big – but I do want you to have legitimate expectations.

Your first, second and third songs aren't going to be your best works of art. They just aren't.

There are tons of artists who spent years honing their craft before hitting the big time. Sheryl Crow famously wrote jingles and worked as a backing vocalist for several years before she was recognized for her own talent as a songwriter. Linkin Park have often spoken about the resilience it took for them to keep going in the face of rejection, apparently playing over 50 showcases for labels before they got noticed.

It's the same for everyone, because the art of songwriting takes practice.

It also requires a team.

Be willing to share the load

Rarely does an artist write, record, produce, mix and master their own work.

I've met artists who try to do everything by themselves and honestly, what they produce tends to be a mediocre product at best.

Some artists will even brag that they played every instrument on their track, recorded it on their own and even did the artwork all by themselves. I'm thinking in my head, "Yeah I can tell, you should have hired a graphic designer and definitely had someone else produce it."

I'm not trying to be a jerk, but do you want to be a great songwriter or a graphic designer? There are some tasks as an artist that you should never do. Designing your own logo is one of them – unless you're a designer yourself.

A while ago, I started to dabble with making beats with a software called Fl Studio (also known as Fruity Loops) because it was fun and pretty simple to get started, plus my friend was doing it while writing lyrics. But then I realized I needed to make a decision: did I want to be a great songwriter, or just a good one? A great one. I decided to put my full attention on being a professional songwriter and performing artist.

I don't have the capacity to make beats and produce songs so I hire that out. I'm not saying you can't be both, but I suggest becoming a master at something and hire out those that are specialized in their field.

My biggest hits are always the ones that I co-write with other artists and producers. I find I do my best work in groups of two or three, max. Normally that's two lyric and melody writers, which includes me, plus someone else. Then we hire a producer to make the music, mix and engineer the song.

This is what works for me, and that's something that I've learnt and evolved with over time. You don't need to let not having a team, a producer or knowing any other songwriters to collaborate with stop you from writing and demoing out your songs now.

"The creative process is imagination, memories, nightmares and dismantling certain aspects of this world and putting them back together in the dark." – Tom Waits

Focus on one song

When it comes to writing and releasing your first song you might have demos upon demos to choose from, and hundreds of ideas of songs you could develop.

I suggest you narrow it down to your favorite three or five songs. Then play those three or five songs to some friends and family that you trust and see which ones keep lighting up the eyes and ears.

Lean into whichever song seems to keep getting the best reaction; make that the song you finish writing and recording to a finished product.

Don't think about any of the other songs, put them away for later and focus on just this one song.

You can only promote one song at a time anyway so it's better to have one big slamming song that's epic than a bunch of mediocre songs.

I would rather have two great songs produced and written with a top-notch producer then five to ten songs created with a mediocre producer – just so I can say I have an album.

People don't remember albums, they remember songs. If they remember albums it's because of the hit songs that were on there. Don't let your ego of having an album get in the way of writing great songs.

You want a hit and nothing else.

"Aim for the moon. If you miss, you may hit a star." – W. Clement Stone

Face the fear

I've heard so many great demos and even finished songs from friends and fans and they just never put the song out. They keep saying they're not ready, or they haven't set a release date because they're waiting for a manager or record label to call them back. In other words, they keep putting off their dream.

What they're really afraid of is people criticizing them. They're afraid of what other people will think.

I get it, it takes a lot of guts to put yourself out there to be loved or judged.

But I've found people don't care about you as much as they care about themselves. They don't have you on their minds, they have themselves on their minds.

If anyone judges or makes fun of you for releasing music, it's because your action shines a light on their cowardice. Critics love to criticize that which they wish they had the courage to do.

Do it afraid if you have to – but set a release date and work towards that goal.

"Nothing ever gets done without a deadline." – Manafest

Bite the bullet

I've heard hundreds of excuses from artists who procrastinate instead of releasing music. Some don't think the mix is right, or the lyrics need to be better. Some have simply got an acute case of demo-itis (common in musicians just starting out). I know artists who have waited over ten years to put their songs out, and others who took the plunge by putting their music up for sale online then got freaked out and took it down again. Music is never really finished, just like fashion is never finished. I would love to rewrite some of my hit songs, maybe by rewriting the verse, changing the melody to a chorus, fixing the music in the bridge ... but sometimes done is better than perfect.

If you really want to change the song you can remix it in the future, or re-release it with a featured artist.

"Since you're going to ship anyway, then, the question is: why bother indulging your fear?" – Seth Godin

Songwriting Secrets from an Award-Winning Artist

INSIDE STORY:
The Impossible Made Possible

Let me take you back in time a little, before I had my first big hit. It's 2005 and I'm pulling through the McDonald's drive thru to grab a bite while Adam Messinger, my engineer, is editing vocals we just tracked back at the studio.

I'm with my good friend Trevor McNevan from Thousand Foot Krutch, and we just finished writing and recording the song *Impossible*. We need a food break.

I'd been working on my second studio album, *Glory*, with a spark of hope that this will be my breakthrough album, the one that will reach millions of people while opening the door to fame and fortune in the music industry.

By this time, I'd already released one album independently and one through a record label, but it didn't sell as many copies as I'd anticipated. My hopes really were riding high for Glory, and as I sat in the drive-thru, I felt butterflies in my stomach stirring. This could be the one, I thought. And my thoughts were echoed back to me when I played *Impossible* for my manager and he said, "If this song doesn't blow you up, then I don't know what will."

We sent Impossible to the record label anticipating an explosive response, but all we heard was that they liked it. Overall they thought the record sounded great, but we didn't get any specific feedback.

A couple of months later and with the album release date fast-approaching, I had to push and prod to find out what the first radio single would be. When I heard it wasn't going to be *Impossible* I was super devastated. The record company chose a completely different song, a song which has never, to this day, been a hit for me.

A hit song doesn't do any good for you if nobody hears it.

Cut to 2006, and I'm struggling to get on tours, to promote the album, and to get noticed and find adoring fans for my new music. I remember playing a CD release party in Hot Springs, Arkansas, thousands of miles away from home and from Melanie, my new bride. Just me and my break dancer doing all we could to get the vibe going.

If my memory recalls accurately there were only 50 kids in the audience that night and zero people at the CD signing that had been organized alongside the gig at a local bookstore. (I'm dating myself here a bit because this was back when you did in-store signings!)

The defeat and utter failure I felt on this day really got me down but I tried to stay optimistic and give the best performance I could that night for the fans who did show up.

Months later and I'm still hustling on tour trying to promote this new album that I believe is some of my best work. It was a constant grind and I felt like I was getting nowhere.

The weird thing is that I was on this tour when I found out Glory had been nominated for a Dove Award. It was like I had a foot in two worlds: one where I was exhausted from being constantly on stage doing all I could to connect with fans, and the other where I was shopping for an outfit to wear for an awards ceremony.

In all honesty, on the whole I've come to find award shows boring. But the year I was nominated the Dove Awards were being held at the Grand Opry, and I was nervous as well as excited to be there with my booking agent. While it's fun to get recognized for your work, I'd much rather have fans recognize me than a group full of suits who have their own agenda in mind when it comes to who they dish the prizes out to.

"I don't measure my success anymore by the Grammy's." – Drake

HOW TO WRITE AND RELEASE YOUR FIRST SONG

Even though I didn't win that night I was still glowing from some insanely good news I'd received a few days earlier. That news was worth more than any award.

I was driving down a Texas highway when I received a call from my A&R rep at the record label. (A&R stands for Artists and Repertoire; they're your main source of contact when you sign with a label).

He said he had some good news to tell me.

I was like, "Please, tell me this good news."

"Well, you're selling a lot of records in Japan," he said.

"Really?" I responded, with sparks in my eyes.

As a songwriter it's so validating to hear people say they like your songs, but to hear that real fans have bought and paid for your music is mind blowing.

He went on to tell me EMI/Universal Japan had imported 10,000 copies of my new album Glory featuring the song *Impossible*, and that they'd sold out in the first week.

"What?! Are you freaking kidding me?" I said.

"So the label imported another 10,000 – and those sold out too."

He went on to say that EMI/Universal wanted to do an official Japanese release with some bonus tracks and that there'd be full press and promotion around the album.

At this point I was freaking out, doing all I could to stay cool and calm.

And it turned out the song that they really loved was *Impossible*.

They said I sounded like Linkin Park meets Eminem, calling me 'the one-man Linkin Park'. I was honored and humbled by these comparisons.

HOW TO WRITE AND RELEASE YOUR FIRST SONG

The label wanted a music video filmed for *Impossible* as soon as possible, no pun intended, but with one caveat – a meager budget of $5000 bucks!

Thank God I have a good friend who's a phenomenal video director and just happened to have access to thousands of dollars' worth of lights and crazy studio gear.

We filmed a music video on the $5000 budget and made it look like it was filmed on a $50,000 budget. You can watch at YouTube.com/Manafest .

Once the music video was released, sales continued to soar. I had a moment of realizing how crazy things had got when I was in my bedroom studio recording radio liners to be played along with my songs for radio stations all over Japan. They'd go something like, "This is Manafest and you're listening to my new song *Impossible* on Yokohama FM Radio." It was surreal and a lot of fun.

Everything was moving so fast. Understandably, the label wanted to capitalize on the buzz and sales that were taking place. A big promoter in Japan had booked me for two headlining shows in Osaka and Tokyo, and the next thing I knew we were landing in Japan and on our way to sound check.

I remember walking up to the club – I mean skateboarding up to the club because I had to bring my board – and getting recognized in the streets by fans. It was both weird and at the same time a huge boost for the ego. Some fans were even waiting for me outside my hotel as we checked in. Both shows were packed, and fans were singing every lyric to every single song. It was something I'd never experienced before in my whole life.

Not only did this breathe new life into my songwriting career as an artist, but the royalty check from the sales and the songwriting was one of the biggest I'd ever received as a music artist.

"Don't write songs for money, write songs for fans and the money will come." - Manafest

One song changed the whole trajectory of my entire career.
One song blew me up in a country on the other side of the planet. One song still continues to get millions of streams every year, touching people all over the world.

It's always awesome when I find out that fans (and even random strangers) have used my music in their YouTube videos. Impossible is especially popular in this way. One video in particular has these crazy Pit Bull dogs doing tricks – and that video has millions of views. In fact, it has more views then the official music video we created! What's even more awesome is because I own the rights to the song, I get paid off of all those streams generated on YouTube.

HOW TO WRITE AND RELEASE YOUR FIRST SONG

Impossible was written by three young guys in a home studio with only one goal: making great music that touches lives.

I wasn't even focused on the money at the time we created that song, I was much more interested in fans hearing it. I learned that by hiring a great producer and working with other talented songwriters, one song can become an asset that continues to live and generate income forever.

"The greatest music is made for love, not for money." – Greg Lake

Chapter 3:
FILLING THE WELL OF INSPIRATION

"The blank page gives us the right to dream." – Gaston Bachelard

When it came time for me to write my first song as a solo artist, I knew exactly what to write about. Something that I loved so much, but couldn't do anymore because I sustained an injury: Skateboarding. I was passionate about it and I knew the sport inside out. I had a ton of stories I could use in the lyrics and I was fluent in the language and slang of the skateboarding scene.

The song bled out of me very naturally and I had a blast writing it.

Naturally, I wanted the song to be extra amazing. It was my first solo work and the experience of writing it was different to writing a pure rap song, where I only needed to write one verse – now I had to write two.

I was in my mom's basement where my studio was based surrounded by stacks of notepads and pieces of paper all with different lyrics written on them. I was trying to finish the second verse, and it was becoming a struggle. A friend came over and I shared another song lyric I was working on (from a different song) with him, and he suggested I take that lyric and use it for verse two of this first song, making it even stronger.

Full credit to him: that was a really smart idea. Instead of 'saving' all the dope lyrics I'd written I put them into that first song and it was a real game-changer. I still remember that lyric: "I swing the battle axe guillotine your cataracts." Yeah – still dope!

My suggestion is to never save your best lyrics by trying to spread them out between songs. Make each song the best it can be. You can always write new lyrics later and see if you can beat what you've got.

Coming up with a great song title

Having a song title makes it so much easier when it comes to sitting down to write your songs. It's hard to sit in front of a blank screen or page and start from scratch; a title gives you something to bounce off.

I was interviewing my friend Sam Tinnesz for my Fighter radio show and he stayed a little longer so I could ask him some questions about songwriting. Sam currently has over 3 million monthly listeners on Spotify and it seems like every week he's got a new song featured in a TV show, movie or video game, so I really wanted to pick his brains on how he titles his tracks so I could share his insights with you.

He told me that before he writes any lyrics for a song he goes on the hunt for its title. He'll look at book covers and movie titles for that one word or phrase that triggers a song title for him.

Here's the thing: it's the song title that really sums up what the song is about. It gives listeners a window into the song before they hear it.

Once you have your song title, which in many cases can be used in the chorus, you have one of two choices.

#1 – Start writing the chorus pulling inspiration from the title. This can always be edited, changed and edited more until you're happy.

#2 – Write verses that lead the listener on a journey towards the chorus. I have a song called *Human*, and in the verses, I share about the mistakes I made in my relationship with my wife and how sorry I am. The verses are leading the listener and eventually pointing to the chorus, which comes in saying, "I'm only human."

Stars and Boom: Two awesome titles

My friend and Grammy award-winning producer Adam Messinger gave me the best songwriting lesson of my career when he pointed out why he admired Switchfoot's hit song Stars.

He energetically shared how in the verse, the lyrics speak of being down and out and going through struggle, and how that leads and builds to the chorus where the band smashes in with this line, "But when I look at the stars…" which is repeated several times, with the emphasis on the word 'stars'. That's what the song is about. Stars. It's clear, it's memorable, and it's catchy.

A few years ago, I had the opportunity to tour and open up for P.O.D, one of the most influential bands for me when I was growing up. We were hanging out in the green room backstage before their show and I was chatting with their guitarist Marcos who introduced me to their producer Howard Benson. Howard just happens to be a multiple Grammy award winner! He's worked with Papa Roach, Three Days Grace and My Chemical Romance to name just a few rock stars. Little did I know that a few years later I'd be recording a selection of songs at his studio with some of the producers that were managed under him.

Not only was Howard Benson there, but P.O.D's head A&R from Atlantic Records was there too. I was like, "Wow, this is freaking awesome."

The subject moved on to songs and song titles, and specifically P.O.D's smash single, Boom.

Howard said the word 'Boom' was used 20-plus times during that song, so it had to be the title. "That's the song title," he said, "it's in the song so many times – that's what gets stuck in people's heads."

On that tour it was amazing to watch P.O.D open with a newer song that fans weren't so familiar with yet, but to see it still get a decent reaction sparking off the show. Then one night I watched them switch up the set list and open with Boom instead – and that's what the whole place did. Fans leaped off of their feet with fists in the air and hair rocking back and forth.

This made me realize once again how important it is to have a good song title that's catchy, and that works.

INSIDE STORY:
Avalanche in the Kitchen

"What about avalanche?" my friend Adam's wife shouted across the room. We were trying to come up with a word to sum up a song Adam and I had been writing. We'd been working on this song the day before, and we had the lyrics for the verses, the music, and most of the chorus written, but we wanted that one tag line or phrase that would get stuck in people's heads.

We both responded, "Yeah, avalanche."

Adam began to sing "AV-A-LANCHE," saying, "Sure, that will work with the melody."

Into the studio we went, and that should have been the last missing piece of the song – except the verses I had written just weren't sitting right with the track.

I wanted the song to be a mixture of dark rock with a big pop chorus.

The original demo was written to a Fall Out Boy instrumental and my verses were influenced by the singer, but when it came time to sing them in the booth, they didn't feel right.

I tried something else: I rap-sung the verses with a darker undertone in my voice – and it worked – it fit the track like a glove.

Sometimes the lyrics you write can be perfect but if they're not sung in the right tone or performed with the attitude intended, they won't come off properly. At the end of the day the song has to sound believable and a strong vocal performance is everything.

Just to clarify: a strong vocal performance isn't just about hitting the notes like a robot – it's the expressions, tonality and feeling that comes through your voice.

With the new vocal performance we were now satisfied with the song. EMI Japan were hounding us for another record, so we moved on to writing and recording the next song.

The title as a hook

Often, the song title is in the hook. If you look at most hit songs, there's a word that's used a lot in the hook or the chorus and that word is normally also the song title. Not always, but it's very common.

What is a hook?

A hook, sometimes also known as the chorus, is one of the two things: it's either a catchy phrase delivered in a melodic way that gets stuck in your listeners' heads; or it's a catchy guitar riff or other instrument played that immediately grabs their attention.

If it's the former, it needs to be easy for fans to say or sing along with, and it should flow right off the tongue effortlessly.

If it's the latter, it needs to be totally memorable. Some examples that come to mind of guitar riffs used as hooks are Switchfoot's legendary *Meant to Live*, and Guns N' Roses' signature hit *Sweet Child O' Mine*.

When you find your hook, you might experience a light-bulb moment where you'll think, "Yeah, that's the hook right there. That's something I need to use in this song and it should be repeated."

I was finishing a new song called Legendary with my producer Doug and there was this really cool chanty 'oh, oh, oh' he used near the end of the song. I said, "Dude, that's a hook, we need to pepper that throughout the song, not just showcase it at the end of the song."

The beauty of the hook is that it acts like a foundation stone; you can really build your song on it.

Songwriting Secrets from an Award-Winning Artist

IT WORKS FOR ME:
Staying Inspired

"I'll take the dullest pencil over the sharpest mind." – Mark Twain

Here are some of the techniques I use for coming up with concepts for new songs and their titles.

Firstly, ideas almost always take me by surprise. I'll be at the movies, or in church, or hanging out with friends, or reading a book, or driving in the car, or listening to music on the radio – and all of a sudden I'll hear something and I'm like, "That's a song title right there."

It happened to me last weekend when a friend told me a horrific story of how they overcame alcohol addiction. They'd hit rock bottom so hard they'd blacked out and almost died. Their story of recovery touched me so profoundly that while I was out driving in my truck the next day I had to pull over to start writing, and within fifteen minutes I had a chorus.

Other times, I warm up with a mini-research session by playing music to get the juices flowing. I might have a theme or a message I know I want to share, and I'll spend a little time researching the topic and gathering ideas, quotes, phrases. I'll also listen to other songs about the subject, not so I can copy but perhaps pull some inspiration and see how I can write about a song from a different angle, point of view, or tell a different story.

There are so many times I'll hear a song that will trigger a completely different song in me – just because of the way it touches my ears and heart.

Once I get a title or an idea for a song, I start humming melodies and lyric ideas, coming up with different phrases, and I always record them right away. I never put it off because I might forget and then that burst of inspiration is gone.

So often, when I go back to these audio files later, I'm pleasantly surprised by what I hear; usually I've forgotten what I've recorded, and I'm so glad I took a couple of minutes to make the recording.

I've been in countless studio sessions where we've been running on inspiration writing song melodies on the spot – but no one is recording. Inevitably, we quickly forget that awesome piece of music and spend the next 30 minutes trying to recall it from memory. How many hit songs and killer melodies are lost because we weren't disciplined enough to hit record before the writing session starts?

Filmmaker David Lynch once said, "Ideas are like fish." I've extended this metaphor in my own way:

"Song ideas are like slippery fish, if you don't stab them with a pencil they get away."

PRO-TIP:
Always, Always, Record Your Ideas

I have a text file on my phone called 'Song Ideas' and when I go to sit down for a writing session that's often my way in. If you don't have a smart phone or you aren't that technically inclined, just use a journal or notepad to write down your song ideas and lyrics.

Personally, I use my iPhone's voice recorder, because I much prefer to have the lyrics not just written out, but also have the melody sung. It's too easy to read the lyrics and forget how I was singing them or rapping them.

As soon as inspiration hits, whether you're lying in bed about to fall asleep or on an airplane flying over the ocean, you must take out your phone and type out the idea, or write in it in a notepad, or record it into the voice recorder on your phone.

The writer Steven Pressfield talks about what he calls "The Resistance," a force that keeps us from really tapping into our true creativity. Sometimes you just gotta push through that resistance, whatever it's telling you and however powerful it is. Having snapshots and recordings of ideas, lyrics and melodies all help to inspire you and get you into the creative zone.

Open up a document or write in your notebook everything you can think of about the song you want to write. Google different topics that spark your ideas for the song, and write those results down as well, so you have pages of inspiration to pull from when writing your lyrics.

"There's a secret that real writers know that wannabe writers don't, and the secret is this: It's not the writing part that's hard. What's hard is sitting down to write. What keeps us from sitting down is Resistance." – Steven Pressfield

My traveling studio

When I still had my 9-to-5 job I had over an hour commute each way, so I made sure I had a sound recorder in the car at all times. It's my iPhone now, but I would write on the way there and on the way home, all the while maintaining road safety standards and not crashing into anyone!

Never allow waiting time to be wasted time. You can either get ticked off and frustrated that you're in traffic on a long boring drive or use that time to get inspired to write songs without any distractions. There were times I got a little too inspired and had to use my knee on the steering wheel while I tried to type out lyrics or record them into my phone. Luckily, no one was harmed in the making of those songs!

When I did eventually quit my job and make my full-time living touring and writing songs, I kept the same habits. This time my waiting time happened in airports with delayed flights or lost baggage and long six-hour drives to venues for the sound check. I always made sure I had a song I could work on to keep me investing my time wisely.

I want to leave you with this: the difference between the one that makes it and the one that doesn't is he that makes it writes it down.

Be the person who writes it down.

Where to find inspiration

Tap into your passions

We all have different causes that we're passion about, whether it's our faith or a political or social justice issue. My wife and I recently saw a movie called Unplanned, which explores the topic of abortion and the truth about Planned Parenthood. Even though I was a Christian I still wasn't fully aware of the impacts of abortion or why I thought it was wrong. After seeing that movie we wrote a song called Plan for Me which even featured our daughter and went on to become one of my biggest songs.

It can be scary writing a song about something you believe in because you fear you'll get criticized for your viewpoint. But if you don't stand for something, then you stand for nothing. And if you don't stand up for something, then there is nothing for people to stand alongside you for.

I found more people rallied behind my wife and I for standing up, rather than not saying anything. The same thing occurs when it comes to expressing my faith in Jesus; people respect you when you make a stand instead of hiding yourself because you're scared of a little controversy. I think it's possible to approach controversial topics with music but you can do it in a way that isn't offensive. But the truth is the only way to not offend anyone is to say nothing, be nothing, and do nothing – and what artist wants to do that? I say put yourself out there to be loved or hated. Be unashamed. I promise you your hardcore fans will love you for it.

Look to your past or current workplace

I've written dozens of songs about my old workplace, even sampling old voice recordings from there. I can't tell you how many times I've talked about quitting the 9-to-5 in my songs. I think Eminem has a line in a lyric talking about how he used to work at Burger King and spit on your onion rings. I'm sure if you think back to situations that happened at work you can pull some stories out, either that you've heard or experienced first hand. Everyone loves a good story!

Look to your hobbies and sports

I shared earlier that my first song was about skateboarding because it's an arena I know a lot about. Coming from that culture it's no surprise that my songs have been featured in multiple skateboarding videos as well. I had a friend who wrote a song about a famous Toronto Blue Jay player, because he loved baseball so much. That song also just so happened to get featured on TV in some pretty cool ways. That's the awesome thing about writing about your hobbies and any sports you play or follow – they might get used on TV.

I look at Drake and there's no doubt that both basketball and the city of Toronto have inspired a lot of his music. He raps about Toronto all the time because he's very passionate about where he's from and he's unabashed about it.

Use your personal experiences

I don't think I've ever met someone who hasn't experienced a trial, a tribulation, the loss of a loved one, or some kind of emotional or physical abuse. These are extremely powerful topics and stories you could re-tell through a song. I've written about the loss of my dad to suicide many times and I can't tell you how many people come up to me and say they lost their dad too. Your loss could be someone else's hope, giving them a song they can relate too. Rest assured that if you've gone through a terrible crisis there is someone else out there who has had a similar experience. When I got dumped by my girlfriend and hurt myself skateboarding, I chose to write songs and paint the pain instead of letting the pain take me.

Bleed through your stories with music and not through your life.

KISS: Keep it simple, stupid

Sometimes as artists we let our creativity and the desire to impress everyone with our lyrical poetry get out of hand. We start to write so metaphorically that people have no idea what the heck we are talking about.

If you want to write a hit song, people can't be left wondering what it's about – unless the beat, melody and lyrics are so catchy that it doesn't matter what the lyrics are. Having said that, that's really not the norm when it comes to songwriting.

In my early days as a solo artist I played a lot of demos for different producers and multiple times I heard them say, "So… what is the song about?" with a puzzled look on their face. Sure, I may have had some cool-sounding lyrics and a vibe going on, but what I was missing was a clear message.

If you select a song title and get clear on what it's about before you even write your first lyric, it's going to make the songwriting process much smoother.

If you don't have a song title yet, come up with a subject that you think you want to write about. Then Google that subject. Type in 'movies about _____' and that will give you a bunch of titles right away. I use popular phrases, quotes and titles to come up with song ideas all the time.

Don't be afraid to brain dump out all your ideas into a document so you have a ton of content to pull from when writing.

These could be stories, lines from movies, things you've overheard. I sometimes borrow a piece of another song's chorus and use it in a verse. I've also taken an artist's verse that I thought was strong enough to be a chorus and with a little editing here and there I've made some magic.

You often hear writers, generally novelists and screenwriters, say they write by hand before jumping on a computer, and there is some merit in that. By forming the letters with the stroke of your pen or pencil you're activating a part of your brain that allows ideas to flow differently. I personally choose to do this more because I have experienced this creative power many times.

Fact or fiction?

Staring at a blank page (or screen) can sometimes be a bit daunting, even when you've got your title and a sense of the topic or the theme of your song. Writing about your own real-life experiences is a great way to get warmed up. If you're concerned about your privacy, don't worry too much at the early writing stage. The lyrics will evolve over time and you can change anything that feels too personal and make it more universal once you've got the momentum going.

You might also be inspired to write a song based on a true story that isn't yours, and is instead inspired by something a friend or a family member has been through.

Personally, I've written songs that are directly about my own experiences, and I've retold stories from my friends and family, weaving them all into lyrical masterpieces.

If writing about yourself or those around you doesn't inspire you, don't worry. Initially it can be easier to tap into the emotion of a song by reliving an experience, but with practice you can conjure any emotion from a story that you've read, watched or heard about. I will sometimes watch a movie because the music and cinematography stirs up my emotions and put me in a state to write a song. I'll do the same thing by playing songs that I know trigger emotions in me, allowing me to tap into the feelings that will kick-start my writing.

As we've looked at, your principle goal with your songwriting is to tell whatever story you are sharing from the heart, because people have to feel it and believe it.

HOW TO WRITE AND RELEASE YOUR FIRST SONG

Don't try to write about something you yourself are not really sold on. Think about what excites you, inspires you, and ignites you. What are your passions, your beliefs, your hungers? What makes you emotional?

Some of the songs that I've sung hundreds of times on stage can still make me tear up when I perform them, because they are so real to me. This is especially true of my song, *When the Truth Comes Out*, because it holds a lot of deep emotion for me.

Songwriting Secrets from an Award-Winning Artist

PRO-TIP:
Choose One Song

Now there's a good chance you've got a million song ideas you're burning to write about but I'm now going to tell you to choose just one. Trying to write three or four songs all at once is a great way to get overwhelmed, frustrated and be left with four half-baked songs.

I want you to put all your energy and effort into writing one great song at a time. Trust me you'll have plenty of time to write other songs, but right now we want all your creative juices, thought-power and ideas focused in one direction.

Finance expert Robert Kiyosaki defines focus as:

Follow
One
Course
Until
Successful

HOW TO WRITE AND RELEASE YOUR FIRST SONG

If you're still struggling to narrow it down to just one song, then here are a few considerations to help you to choose.

- What song could you write the quickest? This is the one that you are probably most passionate about.
- Which song would be most fulfilling for you to write first?
- Is there a song that has a specific or timely message that would mean a lot to you or others when complete?
- Which song do already have a producer, featured vocalist or musician in mind to help you get the job done?

Use those questions to help guide you as you choose which song is going to be your first.

See which song idea stands out the most and pulls on your heart strings ... and then freaking go for it!

I just want to point out that we're not just talking about writing the song, but completely finishing demoing, recording, mixing and mastering until it is 100% complete and available online before you start moving on to the next song. This takes relentless focus and determination, but you can thank me later when you've got a finished song.

Take all that creative energy and start writing your song!

PRO-TIP:
Schedule Time To Write

If there's a song you want to hear, but it hasn't been written yet, you must write it.

And if you want to write, you've got to schedule the time to write. I recommend you schedule block time: specific times or days of the week where you'll be undisturbed and where all you do is write. And here's the key: mark it on your calendar.

You decide whether it's in the morning, the afternoon, or the night – but block it off on your calendar or something will replace it. If you just go, "Oh, I'll just write whenever I've got time, and whenever it happens, it happens," – that won't work. You've got to block it off in your calendar like it's an important meeting.

Whether it's every Mondays at 6am before the kids wake up or Friday nights after work with your favorite snack and cup of coffee – commit to it. Make a date with you, the pencil and your song journal. Find a stimulating environment that allows your mind to breathe in ideas to inspire your songs.

HOW TO WRITE AND RELEASE YOUR FIRST SONG

Just because you've scheduled it mechanically in your calendar does not mean you will stunt your creativity. I believe creativity comes with practice.

I scheduled a time to write this book for you. I blocked it off on my calendar to write every day for a couple of hours. I don't care if I make big or small progress in a writing session – the point is I'm blocking the time off and getting to work even on the days I don't feel like it.

Apparently Eminem is relentless about the 9-to-5 working hours in his studio. Even if he's just getting into the song and 5pm hits, he's outta there. He has a schedule in his mind and he knows he'll be back first thing tomorrow attacking that verse again. I also respect this schedule because it allows you to prioritize other areas of your life, such as family and your health.

My action step for you right now is look in your calendar, whether it's on your iPhone, your laptop, or hanging on your wall, and plug in the times that you're going to write each week for the month ahead. I challenge you to stay consistent with this until it becomes a habit. I truly believe it will change and accelerate your career.

Chapter 4:
UNDERSTANDING SONG STRUCTURE

"Sometimes I'll have sections that I'm not quite sure how they fit in the puzzle of a tune, they'll get moved around; what I think was originally a verse ends up becoming the chorus, or what's an intro gets dropped as a hook, things get shifted around a lot." – Gotye

That quote from Gotye couldn't be truer in my own songwriting. I will have verses that become choruses and choruses that become bridges. I've had producers say, "I like that idea for a verse more than a chorus," and we'll put the song together like a puzzle.

When writing for Top 40 radio there's a very popular song structure that I like to use, and many artists structure their songs this way.

Here it is:

Verse I
Chorus
Verse II
Chorus
Bridge
Chorus

There are minor ways we develop this: sometimes we'll have a little snippet of the chorus echo before the first verse, and then lead to the chorus. Then we'll have verse two, another chorus, the bridge, and then finish off with an extended version of the chorus.

Let's breakdown each piece of the song starting with verse one.

Verse One

After I have my song title dialed in and I know what the song is about, I'll play an instrumental in the background and speak out different phrases. My goal is to come up with a strong, original entry point into the song. I want the lyrics to start with drama that instantly paints a clear picture of what the song is about when it hits my listeners' ears. I want a gripping opening sentence that pulls my listener in.

The process was slightly different when I wrote my song *Every Time You Run*. When I met up to write with my friend Trevor at his home studio in Nashville, he had a demo version of this song ready. He played the demo and it already had a chorus of him singing with an acoustic guitar. We chatted about what the overall song should be about, as well as how the drum patterns would sound on it. I sent the raw idea to Adam, our producer, to craft a beat and I wrote the verses once I got the beat back. When it came time for me to sit down and write I had a picture of a guy running away from himself, soul searching. I can still remember driving around town playing the instrumental with Trevor's hook and I'd pull over the car to write as I got inspired.

The first lyrics I came up with were these:

"Last night got a little crazy, I don't remember, woke up drunk with the pasties."

Reading those lyrics, you immediately get an idea that I'm telling a story. I'm reflecting on a party or crazy night that I don't remember because I drank too much and woke up with dry cotton mouth.

The lyrics paint a million different pictures with just a few words.

When I'm writing verse one, I'm thinking about two things: what I'm saying and the melody I'm saying it in.

Words matter including how they are spoken!

HOW TO WRITE AND RELEASE YOUR FIRST SONG

"Take my verses too serious, you'll hate me. 'Cause I'm the one to paint a vivid picture, no HD." – Drake

Once I have a strong lead-lyric, I'll sing that part out, either over the instrumental I'm writing or over nothing, and then I'll try to write the next part. I like to sing it out loud so I can hear how each part of the first verse flows.

At this stage I like to look up quotes and try to decide where the song is going from here, and what is it that I really want to say. For example, I was writing a song about heartbreak the other day so I looked up 'divorce quotes' and 'heartbreak' online, trying to find phrases that could inspire a lyric.

Here are the next few lines in *Every Time You Run*:

"My friends say I was tweaked out, passed out on a dirty couch, still in the house. It kinda scares me,

I don't know am I out of control, always waking up still in my clothes."

So what I'm doing there is continuing to tell the story, confirming what happened by the guy's friends saying he was jacked up, sleeping on a couch. This scares him and he's reflecting that his life is out of control: he's tired of waking up in his clothes feeling like crap, so to speak.

Then I begin to share that the guy is so depressed that he's thinking suicidal thoughts, but he can't go through with it.

"I wrote a note that said goodbye to pain, goodbye to shame

But couldn't find a way, I just cry for days

I'm so depressed, soak in wet, I can't rest

These thoughts just beat me to death I'm un-kept."

That's where the verse ends, so the next part of the process is to think of the pre-chorus which will work to setup the main chorus when it comes in.

Pre-Chorus

When it comes to ending the verse it's easy to just rush it and throw whatever lyrics you have at it. Yet I believe in having a very strong ending; you're setting up the chorus so you should make sure the lyrics point to it. When the chorus comes in it should give the song more lift and also summarize what it's about, overall. So the last few lines of your verse are crucial. Make sure they are as captivating as possible as they point to and lead into the chorus.

A pre-chorus is useful for making a final point before launching listeners into your chorus. Not every song has a pre-chorus, but it can be an effective setup for the main chorus.

In your verse, your lyrics will be delivered in one style or melody and the pre-chorus could break down musically, maybe with a slight chord change or a contrasting melody. The contrast could be in the form of parts of the music being pulled out a bit, maybe the drums or other instruments.

On the other hand the song could start off really slow at the beginning and as the pre-chorus comes in you build the music or your voice up with more intensity.

When you're songwriting, remember that the whole purpose is to lead your listeners on a journey. It's the same whether you want them to party or have an emotional response. You create your desired effect with different tonalities and musical landscapes throughout your track.

For the pre-chorus in *Every Time you Run*, I wrote lyrics which pictured the guy reflecting on an earlier part of his childhood with his mom. We pulled out elements of the music on the last few lyrics before the chorus comes in.

Those lyrics are:

"I thought of a song my mom used to sing in church

But it's been so long I can't remember the words."

You can watch the music video for Every Time You Run at YouTube.com/manafest.

This guy feels stuck, depressed and suicidal. He's reaching out for hope, desperately trying to remember a song his mom used to sing in church.

Take a look at your songs and see what you can do to make your pre-chorus stronger. Maybe you can rewrite the last part of the verse to set up the chorus better, or change some of the music leading up to set up the chorus. Think of a basketball player who makes a pass to the guy who'll do a slam dunk. That's what your pre-chorus is doing: it's passing off to the hook for the big payoff. You can't have a big pay off if you don't have a great setup. The pre-chorus is the setup.

"The real challenge of writing songs isn't just writing a bunch of parts - like a verse, chorus, verse - but making something that flows together, that brings you back." – James Mercer

The Chorus

When you're crafting your lyrics and melodies for your choruses, your aim is to create something that people are going to want to repeat. Once you've come up with something, try to imagine yourself at a concert, or driving down the highway singing along. Ask yourself, *Would I sing this? Is it catchy enough? Would it get stuck in my head?*

HOW TO WRITE AND RELEASE YOUR FIRST SONG

Sometimes after I've been in the studio for a while and I'm taking a break to do something else, like taking a walk or making some food, I'll notice if a song we're working is in my head. When that happens, I know we're onto something. If a song you're writing gets stuck in your head, there's a good chance you've got the making of a great hook.

Let me remind you that you don't have to be the Lone Ranger on this. I encourage you to play your stuff for other people. Work with a producer, work with other writers, and get their input. They might suggest certain things to tweak, or offer a melody change, or come up with a harmony. All things that will amplify that hook a little bit more, taking it from good to great. I am always willing to give up a piece of my writer's share of a song to a friend if they can help me take my song from good to great! Because that's what we want in the end.

I always say, one good song can change your life, one great song can change the world. That's what we're trying to do here. It's so important to focus on the hook.

Something we tend to do with the songs I write for radio is to put a snippet of the chorus right at the top of the song. This chorus snippet acts like a little preview, fading in and out quickly. We did that for *Every Time You Run*; we just put a little snippet of the chorus right at the beginning, just so you hear a little vocal fade of the chorus, before the first verse came in. The reason we did that is simply down to the fact that it was the strongest part and the part we wanted people to remember. It gave the song a punchiness right from the start and we knew radio stations would like it.

The Bridge

Lyrically the bridge of a song says the same thing as the chorus. It carries the same message, but you say it in a completely different way. It's like when someone tells a story one way and they give their explanation of how it went down. Then another person tells it from a new angle or perspective. It's almost like the four Gospels about Jesus told by Matthew, Mark, Luke and John. Each tells the same story but from a different perspective. The bridge is that new perspective.

Musically the bridge is a contrasting section or moment of the song that gives release. It comes in after the second chorus only to return back to the chorus. Some say its purpose is to connect the song and extend it, before we pound back into the chorus again.

It's funny as I write this, I'm thinking about why we, as humans, connect the way we do with this song structure. I don't have an answer, I just know it works.

I also know – and this might sound like a contradiction – that you don't have to follow this structure, either. You can format your songs however you want.

You want a crazy-long intro? Try it. There are always exceptions to the rules. The perfect example of a successful group who didn't follow the structure I just laid out and wrote songs that were still super-popular is Guns N' Roses. Their song *November Rain* is over 8 minutes long. Eminem's song Stan featuring Dido was a massive radio hit and it's just under 7 minutes in length. In more recent times Adele's smash Hello is just under 5 minutes long. The songwriters weren't limited by that 3:30 to 3:45 minute range, and people love these super-long songs because they connect with the heart, both musically and lyrically.

But here's the key: it's important to know the rules, then you can break them the right way.

You can be as creative as you want as long as you're connecting with people. That's your goal. That's how you sell records.

Ask yourself, *What am I going to write that's going to change someone's life, despite how I've structured it?*

If you haven't seen *Walk the Line*, the movie about Johnny Cash, you definitely want to watch it. It's super inspirational. There's a part in that movie I love, where he's auditioning with his band. They start playing this old school Jimmy Davis song in front of the record producer Sam Phillips, and it's this preachy gospel song. Sam is sitting there like, "Oh my gosh, someone shoot me. Put me out of my misery," then he tells them to stop playing. Johnny Cash is like,

"What man, what?" And the label guy is like, "I can't market gospel. I just can't get into what you guys are doing."

Johnny Cash has no idea what the guy means or where he's coming from. "What are you saying?" he asks, "Explain it to me."

The label guy's response is, "I don't believe you. I don't believe what you're singing." Then he challenges Johnny with this jaw-dropping question:

"If you was hit by a truck and you was lying out there in that gutter dying, and you had time to sing *one* song. Huh? One song that people would remember before you're dirt. One song that would let God know how you felt about your time here on Earth. One song that would sum you up. You tellin' me that's the song you'd sing? That same Jimmy Davis tune we hear on the radio all day, about your peace within, and how it's real, and how you're gonna shout it? Or… would you sing somethin' different. Somethin' real. Somethin' *you* felt. Cause I'm telling you right now, that's the kind of song people want to hear. That's the kind of song that truly saves people. It ain't got nothin to do with believin' in God, Mr. Cash. It has to do with believin' in yourself."

I love that moment. It's a perfect demonstration of how essential it is to connect with our listeners through our music. And how even an artist like Johnny Cash didn't get it perfect from the start.

HOW TO WRITE AND RELEASE YOUR FIRST SONG

If you want to change lives with your music, connect with your listeners.

"They're powerful, those songs. At times they've been my only way back, the only door out of the dark, bad places the black dog calls home." – Johnny Cash

Songwriting Secrets from an Award-Winning Artist

IT WORKS FOR ME:
Formula For Writing For Radio

When I'm in the studio and I'm crafting a song for radio, especially pop radio, I know there are rules and a formula that I have to follow. If I don't follow this formula for writing a song for radio, then it lessens my chances of getting it played on the radio.

What I'm saying here is veering into talking about song structures, which I'll cover in more detail later, but typically a radio song should be three to three and a half minutes long.

The key element in a song that's going to be picked up by radio stations is that it needs to be catchy. Think about people driving home from a hard day at work, unwinding with a song they can sing along to and connect with. Ideally, radio songs need to have a hook, and a piece of the hook should play at the beginning or hit before a minute is up.

It might sound obvious but the point of a hook is to hook people in. The hook is also known as the chorus. Don't try to be a creative genius here; your aim is to write a super-catchy easy-to-understand radio hit that anyone can get into. Whether you love or hate Donald Trump, his speeches were simple and the language used was at a level Grade 4s could understand. He obviously understands his audience and how to speak to the masses. If you want your songs to win over the masses consider dumbing it down ... without selling out.

The song shouldn't have swearing or too much profanity in it either – or if it does, be prepared to send over a radio edit of the song. If you can get an artist to feature on your track who's already had some success at radio that could increase your chances of getting it played – but don't worry too much if you don't have those kind of connections yet. Just focus on writing a killer song and keep that image in mind of your listeners singing along and feeling awesome.

Chapter 5:
FINDING YOUR UNIQUE VOICE

"The people who are crazy enough to think they can change the world are the ones who do." - Steve Jobs

What I love about music is that it allows me to transform and express myself differently than how I usually am around friends and family. It's a little like how a superhero has an alter-ego: billionaire Bruce Wayne is a businessman by day but at night he becomes Batman and takes on the identity of a vigilante terrorizing criminals.

I've always resonated most with nervous Clark Kent who sheds his clumsy and less confident self to become the confident Superman everyone adores.

As songwriters we have the opportunity to shed our fears, insecurities, and any false or limiting identities we've taken on by becoming whomever we want with the lyrics we write.

HOW TO WRITE AND RELEASE YOUR FIRST SONG

If you were to meet me in person you would see a calm and collected guy. While I'm off stage I'm chilling as Chris Greenwood, but as soon as I grip that microphone in my hand and walk on stage under the glare of the lights – I become Manafest.

If having a stage name appeals to you, give yourself one. But mostly give yourself permission to experiment.

Music allows you to step out and express yourself beyond the boundaries of your day-to-day life. I remember seeing Chris Rock being interviewed backstage and the presenter said, "Man, you're nothing like you are on stage back here." And he looked the guy right in the face and said, "That's because they don't want me. They want ten times me." I was like, "Wow, so true, man!"

Audiences don't want someone monotone and chill; they want someone energetic. They want someone more extreme, someone with a lot of energy. Look at it this way: if you were in a restaurant and you jumped up onto your table, that would be crazy.

But if you were to put that in a movie, it wouldn't be enough. You would need to add more aggression to your movements, or do something even more outrageous.

Think about the different ways you want to express yourself in your songs. The really freeing thing is that every song is different so you can use different monikers and try on bizarre personalities for each one if you like. Don't be afraid to explore the fringes and weird stuff – that's where true greatness is found.

"Do not allow people to dim your shine because they are blinded. Tell them to put on some sunglasses." – Lady Gaga

INSIDE STORY:
The Crossover

"Many Christian artists want to crossover, but don't want to take the cross over." – Anonymous

Some people would argue that I crossed over into the mainstream music industry with my success in Japan. When artists sign to a Christian label in the USA, they talk about wanting to cross over to the mainstream while also attempting not be pigeonholed as a Christian artist. I personally could care less; my faith and beliefs are my beliefs. Crossovers exist in other genres too: there's a crossover when you go from being indie or underground to achieving pop radio success.

Every Time You Run was that song on both accounts. It crushed it huge in Japan, it did hit the charts on Christian radio in the USA – but it was when it hit the Canadian Top 40 mainstream radio that it took everybody by surprise.

When you're trying to get a song on the radio you hire a promoter who has relationships with all the program directors. His or her goal is to get your song heard in one of the weekly meetings these directors have so they'll play it and consider adding it into regular rotation. Sometimes a station will agree to test it out and give it a feature to see if their audience has any reaction.

The radio game is loaded with heavy competition and it's very hard to breakthrough – unless you've got a smash hit and some big pockets. The advantage I had living in Canada is there's a law requiring radio stations play at least 35% Canadian content.

I'll never forget the email that was forwarded from my radio team that read, "Every Time You Run gave Adele's Rolling in the Deep a run for her money."

I was like, holy cow: they added my song that week over Adele's song.

Every Time You Run continued to climb the pop radio charts. As an independent artist who didn't have a major label pushing him in Canada, this was a big deal.

I had old friends I hadn't heard from since public school congratulating me because they heard the song on the radio. It was amazing.

HOW TO WRITE AND RELEASE YOUR FIRST SONG

Artists who tap into their emotion

Take a moment to think about the artists and musicians you admire. How do they express themselves? How do they communicate their own unique voice and style?

I'll share a few of mine: the artists I think are really good at expressing themselves.

The first name that comes to mind is the lead singer of Rage Against the Machine, Zack de la Rocha. The attitude he brings in their smash rock hit Killing in the Name floors me every time. Just a few seconds of hearing him sing I immediately recognize his voice.

That song bleeds through your speakers as he transfers his rage and anger through the lyrics.

It literally makes me want to go and rage out on my skateboard, drive faster or break something.

"Your anger is a gift." – Zack de la Rocha

Personally, I get pretty angry about what is going on in the world today from all the in justice I see. I can let it build up inside of me or I can write a song and try to be a light in this world. You can do the same.

I really admire Alanis Morissette's infamous song Hand in My Pocket; her voice radiates swagger, conviction and confidence. When I hear her sing on that song, I feel like it's coming from the depths of her soul. It's like she HAS to share her message with the world.

Do you feel that strength of conviction about the songs you write? How essential is it to you that the world has to hear the message in your lyrics?

"With songwriting I spend a lot of time living life, accruing all these experiences, journaling, and then by the time I get to the studio I'm teeming with the drive to write." – Alanis Morissette

There's a line in Eminem's song Cleanin' Out My Closet where he says, "I'm sorry mama, I never meant to hurt you." Just from the tone in his voice you can tell Eminem stands behind those verses with 100% confidence. He delivers his lyrics unapologetically and with passion – and that's what makes his songs so magnetic to his fans.

HOW TO WRITE AND RELEASE YOUR FIRST SONG

When you first start writing and singing your songs you might feel silly or lack confidence at first, and that's why it's important to believe every word that you write. You have to sing it like you are reliving a moment so that when people hear it for the first time, they feel like they're right there with you.

There's a movie called The Words in which Bradley Cooper plays a desperate author named Rory who's mission is to get one of his books published. While visiting Paris Rory's wife purchases him a vintage handbag unaware there is a lost manuscript inside from years past.

Rory finds it one day, steals it and publishes the manuscript as his own, selling millions of copies. The actor Jeremy Irons plays "The Old Man" who wrote the book, and when he finally tracks Rory down he tells him, "As I read your book I felt like I was there with you in France, tasting the wine, kissing the girl. Even though I wasn't there as I read the pages I felt the emotions, just like I was there with you."

That's the type of emotion you want to put into your songs. You want your listeners to feel like they are reliving a moment with you.

PRO-TIP:
Breaking Free

If you want to write songs that resonate with people on a deeper level, you have to let loose and break free from any fear that's holding you back from expressing the real you.

In my book, *Fighter: 5 Keys to Conquering Fear and Reaching Your Dreams*, I talk about what a difference it made to my life and my career once I overcame my fears. That's what's going to make you successful with songwriting: you've got to break free of the fear and let yourself go. You've got to get out of that box and let the animal inside loose.

Listen to some of your pre-recorded songs and demos and see how you can put more attitude, emotion or personality to those tracks. Try holding notes in different places, stretching them out, saying them shorter, saying them longer, faster, or slower.

Tweak the way in which you're pronouncing your words. Put a twine and a twang in. Pitch your voice up or down.

HOW TO WRITE AND RELEASE YOUR FIRST SONG

Be willing to try things out and express yourself in new ways.

BONUS TIP: Don't think that adding passion, emotion and energy means you have to be yelling and screaming. Look at Adele: when she sings softly, she does it with extreme conviction and sincerity, and that authenticity really captivates her audiences.

Give your songs your unique vocal print that is filled with authentic attitude, personality and emotion and that's what will set you apart from the needle in a haystack of artists out there.

Songwriting Secrets from an Award-Winning Artist

IT WORKS FOR ME:
Write To The Beat

Before I tell you this story, just know that when I started out I knew nothing about writing songs, I failed music in school and I lacked rhythm and confidence. Luckily I had some good friends who coached me through my insecurities.

Back when I was just goofing around with the idea of songwriting, one method that really helped to inspire me and school me was to change other people's lyrics. I'd keep the melodies the same and even the sound of the words, just altering them enough to feel like I wrote them.

I was introduced to writing my own lyrics from scratch by a guy named Brad who I met through a youth group. Brad was a rapper – the first serious one I ever met.

I was visiting Brad's house one day when he pulled out a 9" vinyl. It wasn't an album but a single, and he pointed out that on one side there was the original version of the song, and on the other side there was the instrumental.

He placed the record on the turntable and began playing the instrumental version of one of my favorite hip hop songs. Then, to my surprise, he started rapping his own verse over the beat – and it was completely different than the original song. This had me star-struck; I thought this was the coolest thing in the freaking world.

He explained his process, which was pretty simple, and this acted as a light-bulb moment for me: he told me you just vibe out to the instrumental and rewrite new lyrics, writing whatever is in your heart.

I'd spend hours in Brad's room going through different vinyl records and writing rap lyrics on the end of his bed. Some beats I really liked and others I wasn't feeling as much, so we'd take turns writing to different beats. The reason I liked writing to the instrumental so much is because at first, I didn't even know how to keep a beat or rap a song over the beat properly. I was so green I didn't know where to start the lyric on the track and where to finish it.

To this day, writing to a beat is my favorite way to write a song because it's easier to find my tempo and pull a vibe from the track. Eminem is another artist who is lead by the beat. He's been quoted saying this about his writing process: "I do whatever the beat feels like, whatever the beat is telling me to do. Usually when the beat comes on, I think of a hook or the subject I want to rap about almost instantly. Within four, eight bars of it playing I'm just like, 'oh, OK. This is what I wanna do'."

As I shared in Chapter 3, I keep files and notebooks full of song ideas, so even before I listen to a track for the first time I might have a subject or a theme that I want to write about. Having said that, once the beat comes on, I let my creative juices flow and am willing to let the music take me in a completely different direction if that's the vibe that comes.

I never try to halt inspiration. When you're in the momentum of writing and creating, your thoughts will generate all kinds of amazing ideas as you write. Let it all flow out of you and worry about editing it later. You want to ride that inspiration train as long as you can before the journey ends.

PRO-TIP:
Working With Rhyme

When it comes to rhyming words together you need to look beyond just finding words that rhyme – you want to make sure you're actually saying something in the lyric.

Don't force a rhyme by trying to fit a lyric into a melody, verse, or chorus just because you like it. That's like putting on a shoe that's too tight. Yeah it looks okay – but it feels terrible. That's the way a song sounds when an artist is singing a lyric that has been forced into too tight of a space. It's better to re-write it, come up with a different lyric or edit so it sings or rhymes naturally.

If you find yourself stuck on a rhyme while you're thick in the process of writing a song, you can just put a placeholder or dummy lyric in while you finish the song and then come back and edit it later in the studio.

Here are two websites I use when I'm writing and seeking those elusive rhymes: Rhymebrain.com and Rhymezone.com.

Also, remember that how you deliver your words is everything. You could have the coolest rhyme in the world and deliver it in a boring, monotone voice that puts people to sleep. Experiment and play with your style of delivery so that your lyrics pack a punch into the hearts of your listeners.

INSIDE STORY:
My First Demo

Back in Brad's room writing my own lyrics over the 9" instrumentals and he says to me, "So, do you want to record that verse you just wrote?" I look up and he's standing there with a microphone in one hand and a blank cassette tape in the other.

I'm like, "Are you freaking serious dude? I don't know about that, man."

I was not ready to hear my own voice; writing my own lyrics was scary enough.

But Brad kept on pushing me and showing me how easy it was, and how I could just press stop and try again if I made a mistake.

I agreed to try it. Next thing I know I'm standing there awkwardly in his bedroom studio trying to find my vibe by bobbing my head and swinging my hands around mimicking the rappers I'd seen on TV. I messed up dozens of times or ran out of breath until I finally got a version recorded that sounded like English.

Songwriting Secrets from an Award-Winning Artist

HOW TO WRITE AND RELEASE YOUR FIRST SONG

I hesitantly played it back to hear my squeaky high-pitched voice (so squeaky that people mistook me for a girl rapper when they heard it later).

Yeah – hearing your own voice recorded takes a lot of getting used to!

At first, you'll think it sounds super weird and awful but the more you practice the more you'll see it sounds just fine.

That way of recording was pretty old-school: from a vinyl player to a cassette with no EQ (audio manipulation) or effects on my voice. It's weird thinking that was about as raw as I ever heard my voice.

Lucky for you technology has moved on and you don't have to suffer like I did! Now on almost any computer you can use software like Pro Tools, GarageBand, or Logic to get your voice sound amazing with some vocal EQs. When I recorded my hit song Human with Adam Messinger, I remember he actually turned the auto-tune on while I was recording because it helped me to find the notes.

It's pretty incredible how far we've come. You can get an amazing sounding demo all by yourself if you or your engineer knows how to work the software in post-production.

By the way, none of the songs I wrote or recorded over the instrumentals were released (apart from giving away the occasional mix tape) because I didn't own the beats or have the rights to them. In that way, anything you do like this has to be strictly for inspiration, for promotional purposes, or to get a demo idea out.

Addicted to beat

After my first taste of rapping over instrumentals with my own lyrics I was addicted. I needed more, but I knew I wasn't always going to be able to drive to Brad's because he lived 45 minutes away, so I quickly got my own record player. Then Brad took me to my first hip hop record store that sold vinyl in Oshawa, Ontario. When you're at a record store or thrift shop looking for vinyl, producers and DJ's call it 'digging in the crates' – it means looking for an instrumental gem to write to. Some producers dig in the crates looking for samples. Brad and I were digging in the crates looking for instrumentals to write our next big rap lyric too.

Most stores would have Techniques 1200 turntables set up in store so you could play the records and decide which ones you wanted. I'd play an instrumental for a few seconds to see if I could catch a vibe and if I did, I'd quickly turn it off.

This is because you only get once chance to hear a record for the very first time, and I personally believe that's an empowering moment. **Audio Book**

HOW TO WRITE AND RELEASE YOUR FIRST SONG

These days, I get myself completely in the writing zone before I turn that beat on and start writing. I'll never get another chance to hear it for the first time and I want to feed off of that initial inspiration. Then of course I'll keep playing it over and over again as I'm writing to it, but the first play of the record hitting my ears is magical.

There was a huge record shop in downtown Toronto called Play De Record which had an enormous selection of records. A pivotal moment came when I bought Mos Def's Black on Both Sides instrumental album. It was almost unbelievable that he released a whole album of instrumentals, giving me so many beats to write to. I saw this as a real gift to upcoming rappers like me, and that's why I eventually started releasing my own instrumental albums so the next generation of upcoming artists can write their songs to my beats. There is a beautiful cyclical vibe to that.

Of course, writing to instrumentals might not be your thing. You might prefer to write on a guitar, piano, or just acapella – which is another method I favor. Even though writing to instrumentals is how I started, I don't always write that way. This is because the beat can heavily influence the vibe of a song, yet when I write acapella without any instrument or guide I find my mind is more free to try newer melodies. Once I have an idea over a track I think is strong enough, I'll then take it to a producer to create my own beat so I can release the song.

Instrumental overload

Over the years my music style has evolved and it has much more of a rock edge to it now. When I first started to bring that vibe into my songs, I began looking for rock instrumentals – which was pretty hard until Napster came along.

I remember being at my computer in my mom's basement, typing 'rock instrumental into the Napster search function. That's how I found the instrumental for *Rollin'* by Limp Bizkit; I played that instrumental dozens of times as I wrote my very first rock/rap song, Freedom.

A lot of my friends at the time were way more into hip hop than rock so they just kind of smiled and let me be the crazy rock rapper white boy.

Then iTunes launched and all of a sudden I had access to a multitude of rock instrumentals at my fingertips. With a few clicks all kinds of famous pop, rock and hip-hop songs came up that I could write to.

Almost every famous artist you can think of had karaoke instrumentals of their songs, from Green Day to Fall Out Boy to Katy Perry. They weren't the exact same quality of production as the original but some of them were super close, and it gave me something I could write to.

HOW TO WRITE AND RELEASE YOUR FIRST SONG

This meant I didn't have to drive all the way downtown to the record store to find the instrumentals I could ever want. In fact, I didn't have to leave the house. This was a revelation. As much as I missed the experience and the inspiration going downtown brought, success loves speed and this got me cranking out more songs than I ever would have written if there hadn't been such an advancement in terms of the way we access music.

These days I just find the song I want on iTunes or Beatstars.com, buy it, and then drag it into Logic or GarageBand to record an idea over the top of it. In fact, this is how I wrote the verses for a song of mine called *No Plan B*. I was in Louisiana on tour with my friend DJ Drue and after the show I wanted to get some writing done. I quietly chilled in the lobby trying to find a quiet spot to write, loaded up a Linkin Park instrumental and No Plan B came spilling out.

I liked it enough to email it to my producer Adam and a few weeks later we had a Skype session to go over some of the recent demos I'd sent. He liked the concept of *No Plan B*, so a month or two later I was standing in his Hollywood studio listening to the instrumental he created for No Plan B based on my demo. I rapped and sang my ideas over it to see if it worked with the tempo or if I needed to re-write it or re-work it a bit. Then I hopped in the recording booth and we began tracking the song right on the spot.

This has been my number one way for writing songs over the years and most producers always thank me for coming into the studio with a demo or idea sketched out.

They love to have something to vibe off as opposed to starting from scratch.

Pull up iTunes or Spotify and do a search for some instrumentals in your style or genre of music and see what pops up.

Play a bunch of them and make a playlist or folder called Song Inspiration, that way you have them saved for when you come to write to later on. Or if you're feeling the wave of inspiration right away, ride it!

PRO-TIP:
Don't Forget To Breathe

When I'm songwriting, I like to do it out loud. I'll sing the song piece by piece, line by line as I stitch it together with my voice. This has two purposes: it's how I make sure it all flows properly, and it's how I make sure I can actually sing it live because it's most likely that I'll be performing it on stage one day or at least in the studio.

New songs always tend to be hard to sing at first without losing my breath because I haven't built up the muscle memory yet. The more you sing your song with intent the easier it is to find your spots where you can take breaths. One of the fastest ways to burn out your vocals on stage or in the studio is not getting enough oxygen by forgetting to breathe.

Other things that help to keep your vocals at optimum capacity are exercise and a good diet, but most importantly staying hydrated with lots of water. Studies have shown vocal cords are one of the first organs to be impacted when we're dehydrated. According to openmic.co.uk it takes four hours for any water you drink to reach your vocal cords so you want to drink plenty of water several hours before a studio session or live performance. The reason staying hydrated is so important is because when we talk our vocal chords vibrate more then 100 times a second – and they vibrate even more frequently when we're singing – especially when we're hitting the higher notes.

"Vocal exercises are the analogy of a runner who stretches before running a race." – Roger Love

Chapter 6:
THE 4 C'S OF A CONFIDENT SONGWRITER

"The nice way to say it is, he lacks confidence."

"Well give him some."

- From the movie Money Ball

A few years ago, I recorded Find a Way to Fight, a song written by one of my friends. He'd played it for me in his studio up in Hollywood and I loved it so much he said I could record it for my record.

At first it was really hard for me to sing it because I didn't write it. I know a lot of artists out there that don't write any of their songs, and they really have to take ownership of that song and be confident singing it. Even though I loved the song, I had to put myself in a totally new head space because the melodies were so different than what I would have written.

When you're in that vocal booth and you want to be confident, you have to believe in every single word you are saying. Think of one of your favorite songs by another artist, one that you've memorized. You can recite all the lyrics without even thinking about it because you love it. Just as much as you believe in those lyrics, I want you to believe in your lyrics.

You wouldn't be reading this book if you didn't have a message or desire to share your voice with the world. If you're going to say what you really want to say and express yourself through lyrics and song, then you're going to need confidence. It takes confidence to be vulnerable and to showcase your talents, leveraging your voice for the world to see and hear.

This chapter is dedicated to building your confidence so you can have 100% freedom to be the most authentic you when expressing yourself through songs.

Confidence is not born, it is built – so let's build some together in the next few pages.

Competence

Being competent at anything comes when you possess the required skills and knowledge to perform a desired task. The more competent you are songwriting the more confident you'll become and that's when you'll push yourself to be even more experimental.

Some of my earlier studio sessions were rough, exhausting and embarrassing because I lacked competence. I didn't have the skills or knowledge of how to put a full song together yet, and I couldn't see the big picture of a finished song. Sure, I could write a couple of verses and a chorus, but I didn't understand the dynamics of a completed song.

I didn't know what backups were, or adlibs, or punch ins – plus loads of other studio terminology that the engineers used.

Thank God all the engineers recording me were patient and willing to help me develop my skills in my songwriter infancy.

I remember one occasion early in my career when I was in the studio working on my material with two other people who were much more experienced than me. I felt really insecure. I was intimidated by my lack of competency and the fact I couldn't add any ideas to the song musically because I couldn't play an instrument. The other guys were both moving so fast I felt I couldn't get involved. Great decisions were being made about my song and I realized I just needed to let the other two guys go at it, occasionally nodding my head and interjecting ideas if I had any (I'm not one of those guys to inject bad ideas just so I can feel I have a voice).

You gain competence by doing. If you want to be a songwriter, write. You're already doing your research by reading this book, but you also have to take action.

It took me years of forcing myself into rooms with people I didn't know and writing songs on the spot to gain the self-belief that I needed. In every session I got more competent and confident, learning a new trick here, picking up a new strategy over there.

Even recently I've found myself entering studio sessions with people more seasoned than me and I always make sure I bring my A-Game. That means I get good sleep the night before, make sure I'm practiced up, and I have a ton of ideas ready to bring to the table.

In his book *Outliers*, best-selling author Malcolm Gladwell put forward the idea that to become a master or expert in any given field, you need to have put in at least 10,000 hours of consistent practice. That may or may not be true; I've certainly known many people who were born with instinctive and natural talent and I've known others who've had to work at it with some serious grit. Don't get discouraged if you're just getting started or if you don't have 10,000 hours of studio time or time writing songs under your belt yet. We all start somewhere.

You might have worked the 10,000 hours but what if you've been alone the whole time? If that's the case it's a good time to move onto the second C of confidence: connection.

"The best tool you can bring to a studio session is a hit song."
- Seth Mosley

Connection

"Songwriting is a team sport." – Manafest.

Song ideas may start alone when in your car, in the studio, or while you're out on a walk, but they aren't finished there. I don't know of many hit songs that were written, recorded and produced by one person. They might exist – but they're a rarity.

Confidence in songwriting comes from connection, from being around like-minded writers so you can encourage each other. Ideas get sharpened with that second or third person who can look at the song from a different perspective than yours. When you work with other artists or creatives, you're tapping into that person's years of songwriting, story and life experience.

A lot of friends and family thought I was nuts to quit my computer job to pursue music as a full-time career. If I hadn't quickly surrounded myself with positive, optimistic and successful artists I might have let people drag me down.

It gives me great confidence knowing I have multiple producers, songwriters and friends that I can call upon to turn any little demo I fire off into a song.

I've attended the ASCAP Expo in Hollywood a couple of times and I always get so inspired by the hundreds of other songwriters who attend. We speak the same language and can talk about things that some of my other friends just can't relate to. Hearing the famous panelists speak is another source of inspiration, especially when they share stories about overcoming incredible odds to get to where they are in their careers.

Even having a connection with my wife contributes to my confidence. I'll share song ideas with her and get her feedback, which I value greatly. My wife isn't just a sounding board; she sits with me to work out some of the songwriting before I send tracks to a producer.

Songwriting isn't a solo sport, it's a team sport. The more you involve other people the more successful and confident you'll become. I regret not getting into more rooms with more producers and writers earlier on in my career because that would have exposed me to more talent.

Having said that, I was scrolling through Instagram recently and saw one of my friends had released a new song. Straight away I decided I need to reconnect with that guy and get him to feature on a song. He's an incredible songwriter with an amazing voice.

Go through your phone and email inbox and make a list of all your connections and set up some writing sessions. If you don't know anyone then reach out to your local Performance Rights Society like ASCAP, BMI, SOCAN etc., and see when the next writer's workshop is.

Finally don't let geography get in the way: I had an amazing writing session over Zoom just recently and have booked further sessions for the near future.

Consistency

I've been a skateboarder for over 22 years and whenever I take a break longer than a week I notice when I get back on my board, I can't do certain tricks.

I have to warm up first. After about ten or fifteen minutes of rolling around I'm able to try the harder tricks with confidence – and I land them.

It's the same thing with writing songs. If I take too much of a break, when I come back I notice I'm not as sharp. It takes me longer to come up with lyrics or melodies because I haven't been thinking creatively. This normally happens when I go into marketing mode for a while, promoting the songs I've written and released. As I write this book, I'm in marketing mode for an album so I'm not songwriting as much right now.

The awesome thing is how quickly the creative flow comes back. After a few writing sessions I'm centered again and back in the zone.

On the flip-side, I also find that when I spend too much time just songwriting I'll need to take a break and do something completely different to refresh the creative juices. A break can come in all shapes and sizes: living a regular family life helps, as does going on tour, or even just having a time-out to watch movies. All of these experiences build up the vocabulary of stories I can pull from in my next writing session.

Being consistent builds your confidence so that when you enter a writing session you know you can bring the goods. This takes time and practice; there's no other way around it until you've got your 10,000 hours in.

I've got over 10,000 hours in both songwriting and skateboarding so even if I do take breaks for longer stints of time I can come back quickly and confidently because it's something I've mastered.

Make it a goal to write every day, or at least every week. Block some time off in your calendar so you can keep developing your skill as a writer.

Commitment

"Commitment is what transforms a promise into a reality." – Abraham Lincoln

Commitment to songwriting means investing your time, energy and passion because you believe in it. You make a firm decision to stick with it no matter what.

When I first started writing songs everything was brand new and fun. All my friends thought my songs were great and it was nothing but applause and encouragement. There were so many of us rapping, singing and writing songs having a great time. But as time moved on and things got more serious it felt like songwriting got a lot harder.

I started to get honest feedback from artists that were a lot more talented than me, and even though they gracefully told me when a song wasn't up to standard, the truth still hurt.

I realized I still had some work to do, so back to the pad and pen I went every night after work.

It's really important not to get discouraged when someone disses your song or doesn't like your idea. My wife has learned to keep her strong opinions to herself when my song ideas are in their infancy and not yet fully developed. As bad as we want to play our new demo or recite our lyrics to someone it's sometimes better to sit on ideas that we're developing a little while longer.

I'll never forget a friend rapping new lyrics he was so proud of to another guy, totally expecting he'd love them only for this guy to challenge him to write something stronger. The look on my friend's face dropped with disappointment and discouragement. Unfortunately, he took the constructive criticism to heart and eventually stopped writing songs.

I've seen so many artists get offended when they receive constructive criticism for their songs and they never improve.

If you want to get into the music industry you better have some thick skin because there is no room for just good songs, only great ones.

Songwriting Secrets from an Award-Winning Artist

INSIDE STORY:
That Time I Followed Beyoncé And Jay-Z

I will never, ever, forget having my song critiqued at a DJ pool by a panel of music industry professionals in downtown Toronto. This was a private event where artists had the opportunity to submit songs for professional feedback.

I had a producer friend warn me saying my songs weren't ready and to keep working at it, but I wouldn't listen. The panelists were just about to get started reviewing the local talent – my category – but one of the record labels first had to preview Jay-z and Beyoncé's new collaborative smash hit *Crazy in Love*.

Talk about a tough act to follow!

Crazy in Love finished and my song was next. My heart almost burst out of my chest from nerves. I felt like the whole room stopped as I heard my unmixed, un-mastered, raw-sounding song played for the entire room.

HOW TO WRITE AND RELEASE YOUR FIRST SONG

When it was finally done the room was silent and when the experts were probed for feedback one of them said, "Yeah, we'd play it. Once." As I began to sink further into my chair wishing I could just disappear a college radio DJ friend of mine said, "We'd give it some college radio love," which was nice of him but not the dazzling feedback I had hoped for!

I just wanted to run out of there as fast as I could, but this whole experience made me realize I had some work to do if I wanted to play on the level with the big boys.

If there was ever a moment in career where I should have quit that was it. But instead of getting offended and angry, I got hungry and made a pact with myself to stay committed to my dream. I'm so glad I did.

It's also worth noting that the song I submitted only had one songwriter and one producer. *Crazy in Love* has four songwriters, and two producers. There is no shame in getting help to make your songs great!

"No matter how hard you work to bring yourself up, there's someone out there working just as hard, to put you down." – Dr. Dre

The truth is, there will always be haters and the more haters you've got the more success you're experiencing. Success and criticism go hand-in-hand. You have to learn how to decipher between honest feedback and feedback from people who are just trying to crush you.

My TV/Film team who pitch my songs to music supervisors give me the most honest feedback for my songs even to this day. Sometimes we nail it and sometimes we miss it.

I may get frustrated, but I don't get offended.

"Offense is an event, offended is a decision." – Steve Furtick

Chapter 7:
WORKING WITH A PRODUCER

When you've written and recorded a rough version of a song, your next step is to find a producer to work with you on developing and recording your material. Make sure you've exported a rough demo to your hard drive as an MP3 or Wav file – that's the format you'll be using when you email your track over to them.

How to find a producer

It's important to work with a producer who has experience and a track record in your genre. Google is your friend here, as is Instagram, YouTube and Spotify. Their previously produced songs are their references.

Start building a list of the producers you'd like to work with, based on the genre of your music, the quality of their work, your budget and their availability.

You also want to know if they're the ones responsible for making the tracks they've worked on great. Be careful you don't hire the guy who just happened to be in the room engineering the song, or pressing record, or the producer who made the arrangement. Normally there is a driving force behind a hit record, and you want to make sure you hire that guy. Furthermore, find out who mixed the songs they've produced, and if mixing is included in the prices they quote.

When it comes to money, I typically pay a 50% deposit and then the other 50% once the song is finished – that way everyone is motivated to get it done. Never pay 100% up front. Make sure all terms are agreed to regarding publishing, points, fees and deadlines before exchanging money or work is done. I've heard all kinds of horror stories of artists not receiving their masters or files. Thank God after 20 years in this business I have never had a bad experience with a producer.

Next, start emailing the song out to the different producers on your list. If you don't have their contacts, do a Google search. Jump on LinkedIn and Instagram and DM them if you have to. You can also look up other artists they've worked with to ask if they would be happy to give you their contact details or to introduce you to them. People are a lot easier to get a hold of than you think, but you've got to be relentless. Your email should be short and to the point. This isn't the time to tell them your whole life story. They don't care.

The email should be as simple as this:

> *Hey [First Name]*
>
> *My name is Chris A.K.A Manafest, I'm a Rock artist from Toronto Canada.*
>
> *I love the songs you produced for [Insert Artist Name].*
>
> *I'd love to work with you on one of my upcoming singles and wanted to see what you charge per track and what your availability is in the next couple months.*
>
> *Here's one of the ideas I was working on:*
>
> *Link to the song (never attach a song)*
>
> *Let me know what you think and I look forward to hearing from you!*
>
> *Chris*

If you don't get a response within three to four days, then follow up again politely with something like:

> *Hey man, just wanted to make sure you saw this email. I know you're busy but would love to work with you on my new single.*

Then paste the rest of the original email underneath.

You should follow up at least three or four times in total, and maybe message them over Instagram, LinkedIn or Facebook – but always be polite and courteous. If you don't get a response, move on to the next producer. Maybe you can work with your first choice on a different song in the future.

Check the small print

Once you get a response from a producer who agrees to work with you on your song, you'll want to be clear on what the terms of the contract are.

You'll want to know if the production fee includes mixing and mastering, or just production. You'll also need to know how much publishing they want, whether it's 50/50 or 60/40 – that's especially important if you've already written most of the music and lyrics yourself. I've rarely ever had producers ask for points (a percentage of the master royalty sales) on top of publishing I prefer to pay a higher production fee so I'm not paying out any points, simply because I don't have the in-house accounting team to be handling that type of paperwork. Companies like Distro Kid and Stem do allow you to pay out master royalties to different parties which makes it easier on the accounting side, but I still prefer to keep things clean as possible. TV/Film writing is the exception here, where it is common the producer and songwriter split everything 50/50 in terms of master rights and publishing.

In my experience most great producers are also good mix engineers but that isn't always the case. Sometimes I'll have to pay someone anywhere from $1000-$10,000 to produce, record and write the music for a song, then pay an additional $500 for a good mix engineer, and a further $100-$200 to have someone master it.

These aren't exact numbers, your producer could charge more, or they could charge less, depending on their experience and their reputation. Obviously you'll have to pay more if the person is a Grammy-nominated producer with a stellar track record.

In my opinion, you get what you pay, but always check their work: just because someone commands high rates doesn't mean they're great at what they do. Check their most recent work and don't be in such a rush that you hire someone just to get the job done.

Once you agree to work together, it's always a good idea to agree to a schedule that suits you both, and set a deadline for when the song will be finished.

Lately I've been working with a lot of producers over the internet to write the song, the music, and the lyrics, but there is nothing like being in the same room and feeding each other's energy and vibe for inspiration. However you work together, I recommend you send your demo idea ahead of time so the producer can get started on the track before you meet up.

"You never know when you're going to be doing your best work. Be willing to experiment." – Rick Rubin

Songwriting Secrets from an Award-Winning Artist

IT WORKS FOR ME:
Why I Don't Memorize Lyrics Before I Hit The Studio

I stopped memorizing my lyrics before a studio session years ago. Back in the day, when I booked my first studio sessions, I would want to have my lyrics completely memorized. This helped me to be more confident and it meant there was less time wasted and fewer re-takes required.

The problem was, when I got to the studio, the producer I was working with would want to change a melody, or rewrite part of a verse, or add to the chorus.

When I then stepped back into the vocal booth after we made the changes, I'd start to sing the old version of the song, because I knew it so well and had practiced it so many times. I had real trouble trying to rewire my brain, and it made it hard to improvise and for new creative ideas to be born.

Now I no longer memorize my lyrics. We'll print them out in the studio so we have them there to reference, but the process has become much more fluid and dynamic. Sharing the lyrics with my producer as a Google doc is also helpful, because it allows us to edit and see the changes we make in real time. I really like this loose way of working; being able to effortlessly switch lyrics and melodies on the fly is really freeing.

As an artist it's important to be versatile and know that nothing is set in stone. Understand that trusting the process in this way does take practice, and your skills as a songwriter will develop the more you write with other people.

Recording day: what to expect

Where you start from depends on whether the two of you have been hashing out ideas over email or conversing before you get into the studio. You might arrive with a version of your song that's been edited a little more than the last time the producer heard it, and there's a good chance there still might be more editing to do, or lyric changes, or possibly a rewrite of the whole thing. It varies, depending on where things are at.

I recently wrote a song called *Dangerous* with a producer friend of mine. I had initially sent a couple of ideas over to him with a verse and chorus, and our objective was to write a song for TV/Film. However, when he started working on the track, I quickly realized my lyrics wouldn't fit. I thought the track was so dope that I started writing new lyrics right there instead of trying to force my old lyrics on top.

You can't be too attached to your lyrics or any of your ideas. You always have to do what's best for the song.

When I first started writing songs, I would have probably have been super intimidated about rewriting two verses in a couple of hours, but you've got to give it your best no matter what.

If the producer is a seasoned professional, they should be able to help guide you with the recording process and help you to see the big picture of the song. For years my producer Adam Messinger would guide me in developing a vision for the whole song we were working on. Sometimes his brain would work so fast he'd map out the entire song before I had a chance to give much more of my own input. His ideas were always dope so I'd never object.

If it's your first time recording in a studio then you're probably going to need to book two days of recording because the first day might be spent rewriting, with the second day spent tracking the vocals. Don't get frustrated if it's your first time, understand it's a process and have fun with it. Don't let your ego get in the way of rewriting the best song you can.

"Songwriters usually think their most recent song is the best one they've ever wrote." [Laughs] - Pete Seeger

PRO-TIP:
In The Vocal Booth

Let me be your virtual vocal coach for a second and share some advice for being in the vocal booth that's served me well over the years.

First, it's always best to record when you have the most energy so you can give the best performance you can. That doesn't mean yelling or shouting, it's much more nuanced than that. If your energy levels are high, this will assist the engineer in pulling the best performance he or she can out of you.

'Best performance' obviously means different things to different genres of music. If it's a hype song, it's about making sure you've got that swagger on and that style. If it's a more tender or emotional song, it's about making sure your voice has that emotion and texture to it.

In essence, it's about being in the right mindset so you can project yourself into the song.

I track a lot of vocals at home these days and I make sure I do it when I'm in a good headspace, and not distracted or thinking about other things. If you record at home, put your phone on airplane mode and stop checking email or looking on social media.

The only thing I want you to think about is how you can best stir up the necessary emotions by tuning in with what you're singing about, so you can really feel the song.

The bottom line is this: if you're not feeling it when recording it, I can guarantee the listeners won't be feeling it when they listen to it. They'll hit skip or turn you off.

Items to have close by: a bottle of water, your lyrics, and maybe a cup or flask of tea if you're singing and really pounding it out. Take breaks in between takes so you don't smash your throat and vocals chords.

Clear your mind and stay focused on the song because sometimes you're going to be doing take after take. The producer or engineer might say, "Hey, you were a little pitchy. Review that one part again." And they might do a punch-in and replay the track and you'd better be ready to punch that part on the spot. (Punch in means to re-sing a part of the lyric.)

Some people are against the punch-ins. Some aren't. I think it's all about getting the best song you possibly can. If you have to punch in on a certain lyric – for example if you sing the first part of your lyric and then you mess up the second half of it – you have to punch in a certain spot. The goal should be getting the best sounding performance that you possibly can.

The producer might say, "Hey, you gotta do that whole thing again, because the beginning part was good but at the end you were off a little bit." Or maybe, at the very beginning, when you first started to sing the lyric, you didn't really have the energy, but you started to pick it up at the end. So, they're like, "Hey, give me that energy that you gave me at the halfway point of that lyric, at the very beginning."

The point is – it can feel relentless. But it has to be. It's an uncompromising process, because if you compromise your song won't be the best it can be.

Sometimes we'll track the chorus first and then hit the verses, but after recording the verses I'll find I'm more warmed up. So we'll go re-track the chorus and get an even better performance because now I know the track, I have the whole song in my mind, and I can punch in more confidently.

Confidence is everything when singing because you can instantly hear in someone's voice if they're comfortable or not. Confidence is the difference between the singer who smashes like a guy doing a cannon ball into a lake or the one who just dips their little pinky toe in the water to see if it's cold. You can't be dipping in your little pinky toe in when it comes to tracking vocals.

You got to be all in baby!

Once the producer feels like they have enough good takes and the song is coming together, your job is almost done. There might be some backups, adlibs, or harmonies to add afterwards. Plus you may want to get a featured artist or guest instrumentalist on the song depending on what your objective is.

The edit and the rough mix

Depending on your producer's schedule and what timeline you've agreed to, it may take a few days or a couple weeks until they get back to you with a rough mix of the song. It often takes time to edit and tune your vocals to make the track sound awesome – so be patient! At the same time, don't be afraid to follow up and say thanks and that you can't wait to hear what you guys recorded. Always stay upbeat and excited as opposed to coming across with attitude or complaining.

Your producer will either send you a first rough draft of the song, or it may come back pretty much done. The last email I got from a producer I worked with read, "Are you ready to freak out??? Cause this sounds like 🔥🔥🔥" The song was attached to the email, and

HOW TO WRITE AND RELEASE YOUR FIRST SONG

he was clearly excited about it. I responded with, "Sounds insane man! Send it to the TV/Film company and see what they think."

Sometimes you are going to love the song right away and it will require very few changes or feedback. Other times you may have a ton of changes or edits you'd like made. You might not like the mix, or you might not be fully into how the music sounds in certain parts, or how you sound on a specific verse or chorus.

If you get the song back from the producer and it's totally missed the mark, don't panic, just keep working at it until it gets finished.

Whenever I have feedback to fix a song, I always email back something positive with my suggested changes.

Here's an example.

> *Hey Man, sounds great and love where this is going. Here are a few of my notes:*
>
> *1) Can we turn the vocals up a bit in the verses, they're being drowned out?*
>
> *2) The drums specifically: the snare seems a little hot if we can turn that down.*
>
> *3) Right before the chorus comes in can we add some music, so it builds and the chorus smashes?*

> 4) Not sure if the chorus is strong enough, I think we may need to rewrite something.

That's all I got for now man, let me know what you think.

Any professional producer worth his salt will NOT get offended. His job is to make you happy and create the best song possible. That is of course if your requests aren't crazy off the wall and you don't keep changing your mind every second.

The final mix

When you're happy with the song, it's time to get it mixed. It might be the case that your producer also includes this service as part of his production fee – if they do, make sure you listen to the mixes before you agree on this, because not all producers are great at mixing. A great song that is poorly mixed ruins the whole thing.

If you're hiring a separate mixer, do your research and get some references and names, but most importantly listen to multiple songs they've mixed so you can compare. I have a buddy who always gets hired for the job to mix records because other mix engineers only ever get the song 80% of the way. There's always something missing. Sometimes you can't even put your finger (or should I say ear) on it – but you know something's not right.

That's the talent my friend has. He can take it that last 20% of the way which makes all the difference. In this cutthroat music industry, you can't afford not to get your songs mixed properly; make sure you budget accordingly for it.

Mastered

My first few records which sold hundreds of thousands of albums were mixed and mastered by the same producer. Then as I worked with other producers, they'd send it out to get mastered by a specific mastering house or engineer. As long as a song is mixed well and already sounding awesome, there isn't much the mastering guy does to make it that much hotter. To my ears, at least.

Having said that, when it comes to producing an album, making sure the songs are all the same level is super important and I find great value in that.

Hire a mastering guy, but make sure he doesn't blow your levels so the song isn't peaking and blowing up speakers. You should be paying anywhere from $100-$150 a song for mastering; anything more than that I don't think is necessary.

Release date

Congratulations – your song is finally done! It's mixed, it's mastered and it's sounding awesome. You're ready to share it with the world, and I know you want everyone to hear it as soon as possible. However, this is where you need to take a pause and schedule a release date. Make the release date at least a few weeks to a month in advance so you can plan your marketing.

If you're not strategic with this, you run the risk of being extremely disappointed in the results. You need to create a plan to market the song. I have many courses and books on marketing and releasing your songs: *Spotify Profits, YouTube Playbook, and Music Marketing & Promotions Guide*. I suggest you read all three before you release your song. You'll also find some condensed and direct advice on how to market your music in Chapter 10 of this book.

Think about it: it would be such a waste of all those long nights, blood, sweat, tears to not launch your song properly to the rest of the world. You want this song to come out with a bang, not with a puff or to the sound of crickets. So be patient and put together a strategic marketing plan to blow this song up.

PRO-TIP:
Pay For Professional Artwork

Although we're advised not to, the truth is people *do* judge a book by its cover, and that also goes for our songs. I always tell my Fanbase University students that fans don't hear you first, they see you first.

As they scroll through Spotify, Apple Music, or YouTube, it's the thumbnail that grabs their attention.

Think about how you scroll through Netflix trying to choose a movie: you click on the thumbnails that seem most interesting to you. How many great movies have we skipped over because the creator didn't spend a little extra care on the cover art?

Your artwork needs to wow people on the first glance and match the style of music genre you're in. If the cover looks cheap and like no effort was put into it then browsing customers will assume the same thing about the way it sounds. You only get one chance at a first impression, so let's create something that stands out from the crowd.

You'll want to hire a graphic designer who specializes in music artwork covers. There are some websites like Fiverr.com and Upwork.com where you can get some great work done for a decent price – but don't cut corners in quality. Be diligent about who you hire: make sure you see samples of their work, and when you're communicating ensure that they 'get' you and what you're looking for before you hit the hire button.

You've spent countless hours on your song, both on your own and with your producer. It makes me cringe to see an artist whip a cover in a day and approve not recognizing this crucial part in the songs release.

"A great package on a great product creates an explosive reaction." – Ryan Holiday

This is also a great time to get a logo designed for your artist or band name. I've had multiple logos designed by my wife, Melanie, at Visioncity.biz studio. She's designed the majority of my album and single covers.

Some people think you have to be on the cover but that's not always the case. We've used creative photos from our own archive of shots over the years or we've grabbed high resolution photos from Unsplash.com or Pexels.com. We've used these website heaps of times to get great photos that can be used free of charge, and you don't need to ask permission or provide credit to the photographer – although they appreciate it if you do.

You might opt to hire a local photographer to do a photo shoot with you to get some great images that could be used on the cover. If you plan on releasing an album it's a good call to get some extra photos taken for press releases, and you can also use some of these photos throughout the album's artwork.

I currently use a digital distribution company called DistroKid which allows artists to upload and distribute their music in over 150 digital stores and streaming services across 100+ countries worldwide.

Here's the requirements checklist for images they accept. I'd expect most digital distributors to have a similar checklist.

> *File Type: JPG, PNG or GIF image File. File must be in RGB mode, even if your image is black and white.*
>
> *Image Size: At least 1600x1600 pixels in size. iTunes recommends files be 3000x3000 pixels*
>
> *A perfect square.*
>
> *No blurriness, pixilation or white space.*
>
> *Title and artist must match the release exactly. Any featuring artists you put on the artwork must be credited in the release information.*

No extra information or labels.

No social media links, contact information, store names or logos, pricing information, release dates, "New" stickers, etc

Chapter 8:
THE TRUTH ABOUT LABELS

(Short Answer: You Don't Need One)

Until recently, there was a lot of stigma towards independent artists releasing songs on their own without the backing of a label. Recent technological innovations have helped to break down these walls and take power away from the gate-keepers – and this is a really awesome development, in my opinion.

The advent of Spotify, along with amazing digital distribution companies like TuneCore, CD Baby, and DistroKid, has opened the whole industry up and democratized it. With a push of a few buttons, artists can upload their newly-recorded songs to Apple Music, Amazon and Spotify within 72 hours.

This has leveled the playing field for songwriters and artists, making our music available to people all over the world. It's also enabled artists to keep 100% of their royalties and publishing without giving it up to the labels.

HOW TO WRITE AND RELEASE YOUR FIRST SONG

The only drawback to this is that there's a lot more competition, with tens of thousands of songs uploaded online daily.

But as the saying goes, the cream rises to the top. I believe with a hit song you have just as good of a chance as any label artist at growing a massive audience with your music.

You don't have to have a record label in order to release your songs, unless you like giving away control and a huge portion of your rights.

MYTH-BUSTING:
Four Reasons Why It Makes Sense To Go Independent

There are numerous reasons why artists are choosing the independent route while record labels are going out of business.

Here are four reasons why it makes sense to stay independent:

#1 - You keep 100% control of the master of the song plus your publishing.

#2 – If you put an album out with a label, they'll market you for two weeks but if it doesn't sell, they stop marketing you and you're forced to market the album yourself. To be clear, that's an album on which you only receive 20% of sales (if that) after they recoup. It's common to hear labels refer to artists as spaghetti: they sign a bunch of artists, throw them up to the ceiling and see what sticks. No thanks; I don't want to be anyone's spaghetti experiment.

#3 - It can take years to sign with a label and then schedule a release date, but if you release it yourself you are in 100% control of when you want to get your record out there.

#4 - When you're a new songwriter who isn't yet established, it's hard trying to chase down a record label with no sales or radio history, and you're not in a very good position to negotiate. It's much better to have the label seek you out instead of you chasing them.

If you build your career on your own, developing relationships as you go and getting to know a network of people in the industry, you can have just as much success without a label – and you don't need to give up any rights to your songs.

It always makes me sad when I notice massive hit songs that are continuing to get millions of streams per year, but when you look who owns the song you see it's one of the major label names like Universal, Capital, Sony ATV etc. This means that label owns it, most likely forever, and the artist is getting very little if any of the royalties.

Get in the mindset of having a long-term career. Don't think in terms of just one and five years from now. Think in terms of decades – because that's the kind of long-lasting impact and relevance your songs can have. Ryan Holiday, in his book Perennial Seller, beautifully encourages creatives to make something that can stand the test of time.

"You can now be a master of your own destiny. I'm not sure why you would sign up with a record label." – Sean Parker (Founder of Napster)

Songwriting Secrets from an Award-Winning Artist

PRO-TIP:
If You Do Sign With A Label – Keep Your Publishing

The majority of the songs I write are with one other person. As the artist Manafest, I pay for my albums to be recorded and I pay a producer his fee so I own 100% of the master side. I then sell the album online via Apple Music, Spotify etc. I own all sales of the master side 100% because I paid for the recording and own that copyright.

But before I was independent, the first record label I signed with was BEC in the USA, and the deal did not include me giving up a big portion of my publishing. Without getting too technical, music publishing concerns songwriters and copyrights. Whenever your song is sold, streamed, licensed or publicly performed at a show or on TV, the songwriter and copywriter is owed royalties.

There is a royalty generated on the master side of the song, which is normally paid to the record label or to you or your band if you're an independent artist.

The second royalty that is generated is the publishing or songwriter royalty for whoever contributed to the writing of the song.

The original deal I signed with BEC was a licensing deal where they could exclusively sell my record for seven years and then I'd get the albums back. This deal didn't include them owning any piece of my publishing – only the copyright side from the master.

When I got big in Japan, I had a good lawyer who advised me to sign just a publishing admin deal with Sony Japan. That ensured I got paid for all the radio airplay, music videos and sales that took place overseas. They didn't own any of my publishing, they just administrated and collected on my behalf, taking a 20% cut – which was much better than signing over 50% to a record label in perpetuity.

Don't let some label try and steal your publishing – especially if they aren't going to do anything to help you sell more records or get featured in TV and films. I'm fine with sharing a piece of the publishing pie – but only if the pie is bigger because we're working together. I'm not interested in labels who just want to cut into my own pie and not bring any extra pie to the table.

By the way, that word perpetuity means forever, and it's often used in contracts in the entertainment industry. Always get an entertainment lawyer to look over any contracts you're considering signing. I'll talk more about record deals in my upcoming book:

What every artist wished they knew before they signed a record deal.

"If you're going to give up any of your publishing, then let it be with a great songwriter who can turn your song into a hit." – Manafest

INSIDE STORY:
Fool Me Once

When I signed away the rights to my songs to a label for seven years at a time, they had me thinking I was working for them. And I was. But I had this idea that I had to impress them by touring my face off and investing my own money into promotions, videos and buying onto tours. I didn't even get an advance *and* they reaped almost 100% of all the royalties. Thank God, the deal I signed was a licensing deal, so although the label did own my music for seven years (when the majority of the sales were made), at least once the seven years were up, I owned my music again for a lifetime. Now, when I promote my music, I benefit from the hard work I put in.

No one is going to care about the songs you write as much as you, so take responsibility for them and don't sign them away for a pittance.

As an independent artist and songwriter, you can hire your own publicists, radio team, music director and pay for online promotions to help make your songs successful. Don't feel you need to bow the knee to a label or the first guy in a suit with a record contract who shows any interest.

My friend Sonny from P.O.D is a great example of someone who saw that waiting patiently for the right deal was way better than just signing a deal for short-term gain.

I advise that you trust the system I'm laying out for you in this book. Take it step-by-step to ensure your song goes from idea to demo, to recorded, to released.

"I've had big record label presidents look me in the face and say, 'Your music sucks, you don't know who you are, your music is all over the place, and we don't know how to market this stuff. Pick a lane and come back to us.'" – Bruno Mars

Back when I was on my first tour of Japan, I came to an agreement with my A&R that once my deal was up with my label in the USA, I'd sign with them directly in Japan and cut out the middleman. This sounded great to me because, honestly, the label in the USA were extremely lucky because it was the A&Rs in Japan who really pushed me and my music. The label in the USA did nothing for me and just jumped on the coat tails of the distribution and sales that were rolling in from Japan.

I even remember my A&R in the USA say they tried pushing some of their bigger USA acts to Japan but they didn't want them, they wanted Manafest!

With the help of my friend Adam Messinger and his Hollywood connections, we tried to find a major label who would sign me and release my new record, The Chase. But because Japan needed the record turned in for the street date of the release, we needed to find a US distribution partner fast.

I ended up signing another deal in the USA with the same label as my previous albums, but this time they only had rights to the USA, not Japan or any other countries. I was told the president of the US label was furious about us cutting them out of Japan, but they liked the new record so much they agreed to release it in the USA.

Hometown hero

When *The Chase* was released in Japan it was a massive success, selling thousands and thousands, and I knew we had another hit our hands.

But if I'm honest, I still wanted to have success in my hometown and get recognized on home soil for my music. It's really funny how we can have so much success in one area yet we put our focus on what we don't have elsewhere. Little did I know this was about to change.

I received an email from my A&R in the USA asking if Adam and I could make a radio edit to *Avalanche* because I used the word "hell" in the song. The song lyrics read, "You scared the hell out of me, man." Of course, I was like – sure, we can make the edit no problem, so we changed it to, "You scared the junk out of me man."

This is where a lot of songwriters get their noses bent out of shape and miss opportunities because they don't want to edit their songs to reach a broader audience. I'm cool with edits as long as I don't feel like I'm sacrificing my integrity or the integrity of the song.

What's funny is the in-house radio promoter of the label told me that she said to the president, "That song is a hit and he's cursing in it." The reason it was funny is because I'm a Christian artist and they were trying to get the song on Christian radio, which is a big market in the USA.

A few months later and emails started to flood in on a weekly basis, telling me a new station had added the song, and then another station wanted an interview. *Avalanche* was selling over 500 records a week – which is pretty freaking awesome for an indie artist. It went on to sell over 56,000 singles – not including the millions of streams.

Adam and I hadn't pegged *Avalanche* as the hit song off the album, but it launched me into the stratosphere in the USA.

HOW TO WRITE AND RELEASE YOUR FIRST SONG

Managers and artists began to call me inviting me to open up or be the main support for their tours. I'll never forget playing a show in New Mexico at a High School auditorium. There were over 2000 people and they were all buzzing with energy. We ended the show with *Avalanche* and it was as if we burnt the house down and stole the show from the headliner! I'd had a taste of success in Japan but this was a moment I felt ignited by: closer to home and seeing hundreds of faces singing every lyric to a song I'd written.

Chapter 9:
Becoming A Music Marketing Machine

"Artists think if they write the best song the world will just find it. Wrong."– Manafest

Countless great songs have been overlooked and under-listened to because they didn't reach their audience. Potential listeners never got to hear the awesome track that would become the soundtrack to their youth or be played at their wedding. Effective marketing makes the difference between a song that's remembered for decades and one that sinks without trace.

I wasn't born a good marketer; I became a good marketer

As an artist, you might have hang-ups about marketing your music. I used to; I actually thought the terms 'marketing' and 'sales' were dirty words. They put me in mind of a pushy used-car salesman, someone dishonest who wanted to make a quick buck and didn't care how.

I could not have been more wrong. Now I'm proud to be an honest marketer and salesman of my music.

Once I learned how to market, I really got into it. It gives me a buzz when I do all I can to get my music heard – and when it works.

The truth is, we're all salespeople in some way or another. And, on the flipside, we're all being sold to every day in both obvious and subtle ways.

Someone sold me on the idea of becoming a rapper and writing songs.

You were sold this book, and throughout it I've been trying to sell you on writing the best song possible... *but the hard reality is the best songs don't always win.*

Unless you proactively let fans know your songs exist, they're not going to magically find you.

Even if you're signed to a major label there's no guarantee it will bring you success. There's a lot of behind-the-scenes politics with labels, especially when it comes to them deciding which song is going to be your first single. Then when the single is released, radio stations make a decision on whether they'll play it or not – and that decision is not always based on the quality of your song or whether it's got hit potential – it's based on who they owe a favor to.

What I'm saying here is: a record deal is not a fix-all. Marketing is still essential if you want to stand out in the crowd of talented songwriters and performers.

Don't let the fact that there's heavy competition discourage you. A lot of artists don't have the drive to put in the extra effort in to market their songs – but you do. Right?

Building momentum

When a song becomes a hit, it starts to have a life of its own and gains momentum as more and more people hear it, like it, and share it.

Word of mouth marketing is golden. People trust their friends and listen to recommendations. That's what I love about Spotify: their algorithm automatically shares my songs via auto-generated playlists so they're included in music fans' daily and weekly mixes.

As essential as word of mouth is, remember you're the catalyst behind it. It's up to you as a songwriter and marketer to inject the fuel and promote your song so it gets into people's ears.

Take full responsibility for your song being heard because whether it fails, falls upon deaf ears, or becomes a giant hit – that is one hundred percent on you.

No one is going to be as passionate about your songs as you.

This is good marketing

In the modern-day music industry, good marketing means presenting your music in the best possible light to the right fans.

One way of doing this is to ask an artist who has already built an audience in your style and genre to feature on one of your songs. When the song is released ask them to post and promote that song. Hopefully from working together you'll build a relationship that could turn into an opportunity for you to open for them on tour.

Good music marketing can involve creating a music video that accentuates your song, bringing the emotion to life on screen. Note that *creating* the music video is not marketing, it's what you do with it that's marketing. The video is a marketing asset, you must promote it via online channels like Facebook, Instagram, YouTube Ads and any other platforms available. We'll be exploring those platforms later in this chapter.

Bad marketing is letting your manager, label or best friend handle it all for you. Don't do that. Don't shy away from it, you want to be involved every step of the way to ensure your song is a success.

Good music marketing is staying focused on one song until you've squeezed every ounce of life out of it. Posting the song once and then moving on to the next song is not good marketing!

As artists we are creators and I know how tempting it might be to throw a song out there and quickly move to the next song, and the next song, and the next. But when we do that, we only end up with a catalogue of songs that no one has heard of.

I can't stress how important it is to go deep into one song and promote it for as long as it takes to get a good response. That takes time and patience.

Another important aspect to this is something I tell my Fanbase University members all the time – and it's that albums don't promote albums. Songs promote albums. The key is to choose two to three songs and build massive campaigns around each individual song – that's how you promote an album.

You should have a goal for each song you release in terms of the number of streams, views or sales you want to receive. I made a promise to myself that I wouldn't make another music video until my last one had at least 100,000 views. Otherwise what's the point? It's easy to want to shoot music videos and record more songs because it strokes your ego and makes you feel important, but is it really getting you closer to your fan-base goal?

Write down a big goal you have for your song. It could be a certain number of streams, or a particular artist you want to feature on it, or you might want your song to be played on a specific radio station, or have it featured on a TV show.

And here's the thing: Whatever you spent making the song, be prepared to spend double that amount to market it. If you spent $2000 to record mix and master one song, be willing to spend at least an additional $2,000 marketing it if you want people to hear it and grow your fan base.

Songwriting Secrets from an Award-Winning Artist

PRO-TIP:
Releasing A Song, Step By Step

In my book *Music Marketing & Promotions Guide*, I share the four phases required to hit the Billboard Album Charts.

Right now we're directing our energy on releasing individual singles, so the advice that follows is my method for making as much ruckus as possible for when you release each individual song.

Step #1 - Set a release date

The first thing you need to do is set a release date for when your song is coming out. Unless it's a Christmas song, avoid the Christmas holiday. Why? Two reasons. One: because the major labels release tracks from their biggest artists during Christmas so competition is fierce; and two: it's the Christmas holiday and everyone is super busy with dozens of distractions. I released my album This Is Not the End right before Christmas in 2019 and it was very hard to break through all the noise. Luckily I'd started my crowd-funding campaign for the record in October, so I'd already built up a lot of buzz leading up to the release.

HOW TO WRITE AND RELEASE YOUR FIRST SONG

You'll need a massive budget and super-creative idea if you're going to cut through the Christmas noise with your music. Plus, advertising costs go up at this time because many companies are trying to spend their yearly budgets. So, avoid December for your album release – unless it's a Christmas album or you have a creative way of garnering attention to break out from obscurity.

However, there are other holidays you might want to coincide a release with. National Day of Prayer, Black History Month, and Valentine's day spring to mind. If you have a song that fits into the narrative of any of these celebrated days, then that can be a great way to news jack what's already going on and make it part of the launch of your music.

On the flipside of this, as I'm writing this book right now we're in the midst of the COVID-19 crisis. There's a lot happening out there in the world, including rioting and protests, and I've had to hit pause on a song release. The song in question is called Dangerous, and it's one I co-wrote with a friend. It's geared towards Sports and UFC type shows, and we didn't think it would be wise to release it during this time. Our decision was part based on us being sensitive to the global mood, and also because there isn't much sports programming taking place right now.

Something I've done in the past that's been a lot of fun for both single and album releases is to launch them on my birthday. I tell all my fans my birthday is coming up but I'm giving them a gift – and it's a new song. This also allows me to ask friendly favors of friends, family and fans, by asking them to go listen to my new song on my birthday.

When you've chosen your release date, it's important that you give yourself at least six weeks to promote your song; this allows you enough time to prepare and get your marketing plan in place. Don't set a release date a week from when you upload your song (see Step 2) or you'll miss out on so many marketing opportunities.

Think like Hollywood: movie trailers build buzz towards a movie release – you want to do the same with your songs. Also, you want to give the Spotify editorial team a few weeks to get to your song and listen to it if you want a chance of being added to an editorial playlist. Getting on an editorial playlist can be like hitting the lottery – it's an especially easy way for a new artist to build an instant fan base.

Step #2 – Upload your song

Upload your song to a digital distributor such as TuneCore, CD Baby or DistroKid, and set the release date you've decided on. You'll need a mastered WAV file of your song as well as the artwork. Please review the checklist I provided from DistroKid in Chapter 7.

Step #3 – Call your shot!

Whether this is your first or fortieth song it doesn't matter, I want you to go on social media and either shoot a quick video or share an image (not the cover) and tell your fans and friends you have a new song coming out on [insert date]. You don't want to share the cover because you want to save that content for release day. Sometimes artists get so excited they throw everything out on the internet without a synchronized plan.

There is something about publicly announcing our goals to the world that causes us to follow through more. When we keep our goals to ourselves we're not as likely to reach for them. But if we make a public announcement – now were on the hook and we'd better deliver the goods. That's why crowdfunding campaigns are so powerful – they have a time-stamped deadline and it's a case of fly or die.

Step #4 – Build your virtual street team

Start listing all the people you can email, phone, text and message over social media to tell them about your new song. This is not the time to be the lone soldier. Leverage all your contacts. It's okay to ask for favors, especially if this is your first song or a big release. The message could be something like:

> *Hey [first name] I'm so excited about my new song that released today!!! Could you do me a huge favor and check*

it out when you have a chance? Thanks so much. [Your name]

When I released a big song recently, I sat for hours on my couch direct-messaging my fellow artists asking them to re-post the song to their stories, and the majority of them did. Don't expect people to see your song and re-post it just because. You have to ask – and more importantly – follow up – either to politely ask again if they didn't get around to sharing it yet, or by saying thank you when they do.

Step #5 – Create assets

There are so many cool marketing assets you can create to promote your upcoming song. Here are a few I've tried and tested:

1) *Lyric Cards:* Take the strongest lyrics from your songs and overlay them over photos.

2) *Lyric Video:* Hire a video editor to create a video that has your lyrics over the top of it. You can find amazing video editors for $5-10 an hour on Upwork.com or OnlineJobs.ph

3) *Music Video:* It's not about a big budget, it's more about a creative idea. I've made selfie music videos with a few GO-PROs and they did great. I am currently spending over $250 a day on Facebook and Instagram to sell my music

and we're using a music video in the ad. To learn how I'm doing that visit: https://www.fanbaseuniversity.com

4) Behind the scenes footage / insights: Talk to the camera and tell the story of how you wrote the song and story behind it.

5) Merchandise: We create merch incorporating the artwork from the single cover. As well as selling these products we do giveaway contests designed to encourage people to promote my songs. I use a print-on-demand service for this called Printful.com.

It's your call how many assets you want to create to promote your song, but remember you still have to market each asset. Even with my 27,000 followers on Instagram and 211,000 likes on Facebook, posting a lyric video, lyric card or a music video once or twice is not nearly enough effort. That will barely make a dent to get the word out about a song.

It's important to note that Instagram and Facebook only show your posts to a small percentage of your followers – unless you pay to boost the post, which I recommend you do on the week of release.

Songwriting Secrets from an Award-Winning Artist

INSIDE STORY:
Don't Hire A Promotions Team

Traditional or typical marketing strategies often suggest you hire a publicist or radio promotions team to get your song out, but the problem is you have to commit to spending thousands of dollars up front before you see any results. I've had the personal experience, numerous times, of burning tens of thousands of dollars in the hopes my song would be the next global or viral hit, only to get mediocre results at best.

In many cases it would have been better if I'd hired a film crew to film me setting myself on fire and running down the streets of New York blasting my music out at the same time.

Online marketing is so much more effective, and you get to be in control of it. Also, you can start with a small budget and continue to raise it as you see the impact.

While a radio campaign allows you to track the spins and get a sense of the overall reach of your song, what you might not know is that not all spins are created equal. I hit the top of the Active Rock

20 Billboard charts but had a hard time figuring out why because we had barely any sales. This is what I mean about not all radio spins are created equal: yes, stations were playing the song – but in the middle of the night so barely anyone heard it.

Likewise when a publicist gets you a blog feature or a paid review, do they even show you how many impressions you got? Don't fall into the ego trap of straining to get features or radio ads or even TV interviews – none of these are useful unless they move the dial.

There are zero guarantees in the music business so if anyone is promising you results from a promotions campaign proposal, I would run for the hills like Iron Maiden.

Songwriting Secrets from an Award-Winning Artist

IT WORKS FOR ME:
Using Facebook And Instagram Ads

The best ROI (return on investment) I've ever had for promoting my songs is when I've used Facebook and Instagram Ads. That's because I'm able to maintain control of my budget; if something is working, I can increase my budget; if it isn't working, I can quickly turn the ad off so I'm not wasting my money. Online advertising also allows me to track the impressions, clicks, and shares of my songs without having to be some analytical guru.

"Just how Spotify and Apple Music revolutionized music distribution, social media is doing the same thing for music marketing. Now every artist can have their music heard if they so choose." - Manafest

I'm currently spending $250-300 USD a day on Facebook and Instagram ads to promote and sell my music profitably online. I've had the honor of visiting the Texas Facebook headquarters which are super inspiring (and they have the coolest cafeteria I've ever seen at an office). After selling over 10,000 albums using a Facebook Ads strategy, I was contacted by my advertising rep at Facebook to be one of the first North American artists to be featured in an online case study. You can read it at: *https://www.facebook.com/business/success/manafest/* – and I recommend you do because I think you'll find it inspiring in terms of what's possible with Facebook Ads.

When I first started promoting my music online, I did it by boosting posts on Facebook and Instagram, first spending $5 here and $10 there. I then started to boost my winners: the posts that were getting the most comments, shares and likes. In the simplest terms – If there's a fire burning, then add more fuel to it. If it's smoldering than maybe stop, pivot and try something else before throwing more money at it.

Good marketing will only make bad music fail faster, but you still have to get your music out there to see what the response is.

By the way – if you're not getting any negative feedback on your songs, then it means you're not marketing enough because not everyone is going to like your music ... and that is okay!

There are two types of ad strategies I teach my students for running ads on Facebook or Instagram. They're called direct response or direct-to-sale online marketing, and I'll share them with you now.

Campaign #1 – Give your music away for free

I've taught my students to run ads to a website that gives your music away for free in exchange for your fans' email addresses. This drives discovery and brings awareness of your music to people who might not already know you. I know it sounds counterintuitive to give your music away, especially if you have concerns of piracy. However, for the majority of artists the problem isn't been pirated for our music – it's just trying to be heard. That is often a much larger obstacle, and giving music away for free is one way to overcome it.

The key is, you're giving your music away in exchange for an email address. This allows you to build trust and a relationship with your fans over email. Once you have their email address you can start sending them cool stuff about your music, while soft-selling them on merchandise, or asking for their support on your crowdfunding campaigns, or inviting them come to your live performances.

I always stress to artists how important it is to build the email list. Building an email list of fans is your most precious asset because Facebook, Instagram, TikTok – or whatever the latest social media trend is – can come and go. Look at Myspace – when I think back to all the effort I was putting into that I realize now I should have been building my email list.

Just to put this in perspective: I would rather have 1,000 email addresses over 10,000 social media followers any day. The money and long-term value are in your email list, so start building it today.

I have a free training called the 10x Your Fanbase 5 Day Challenge that shows you step by step how to do this. https://www.10xyourfanbase.com/5day

Campaign #2 – Offer free shipping

This is the campaign that I've used to sell over 25,000 albums online using Facebook and Instagram ads. It's called a 'Free + Shipping offer' where I use ads and my own social media to tell fans that my album is free, they just need to cover the shipping of say $6.97. A lot of artists think I'm crazy and ask me how I'm making money this way. The secret is to have one-click up-sells in place on the page where they add their details, offering them other albums, merchandise etc. Often, people take advantage of these offers, because they already feel like they're getting a good deal by getting my album for free.

This type of campaign has allowed me to promote my music all over the world. It's also allowed me to sell my music both physically and digitally profitably sometimes without having to ship anything. In this strategy not only am I building an email list but an email list of buyers. A buyer's email list is worth 10x that of a list of those who just opted-in because it was free. Both are valuable and worth more than a like or follower on social media, but the buyers email list is priceless. I have another free training you can watch for free that breaks this down at *https://smartmusicbusiness.com/livetraining*

PRO-TIP:
5 More Marketing Avenues That Work

#1 - YouTube ads

If you have a music or lyric video one of the most effective ways to promote it is by running in-stream YouTube Ads in front of other bands' videos. Think about all those 5-15 seconds ads you see before you watch a video on YouTube – they could be promoting your songs. The coolest part is you can target the channels for specific bands if you think fans of their music would resonate with yours. This allows you to narrow your target like a sniper on artists that sound most similar to you instead of taking a broad shot-gun approach where you try to reach everyone. YouTube Ads also allow you to target with keywords. For instance, if someone searches for a band or artist similar to yours such as "Taylor Swift" your video would play as an ad before their video.

It's like virtually opening up for your favorite band, and you don't even have to be there. Bonus: it's happening 24/7 while you sleep.

You don't have to make a full-on music video for this either, it could be a lyric video, or footage of you performing live with the studio version edited into the background. I always tell my students to cut a version of their video that edits out the intro, so the video ad grabs the viewers' attention immediately.

YouTube ads are still super cheap, sometimes as low as one cent per view. It's almost unfathomable that brand-new artists can market their music and get in the game with such a low barrier of entry. I have a whole course teaching you how to run YouTube Ads step-by-step in a program called **YouTube Accelerator** : How to get over 10,000 views on your videos in 10 days.

#2 – Buying onto a tour

Buying onto a tour is like YouTube ads… but in real life. In essence, you're paying to have a time slot to perform your songs as an opening artist at a live gig. The goal is to fast-track building your fan base by tapping into a larger act's audience.

Back in 2010 I bought onto a tour for $500 per show, and it allowed me to play in front of thousands of new fans every single night. This built my fan base and resulted in the sale of thousands of dollars' worth of merchandise. As much as I love online marketing, there is a stronger connection that's made with fans when they see you, hear you, and get to meet you after the show.

When you have a 15 – 30 minute set ready you can start approaching managers, booking agents, or the artists themselves to enquire if they have any buy-on slots for an upcoming tour. The coolest thing about buying onto a tour is that you have a chance to build a relationship with the headlining act and if they like you and you're cool to tour with, they might invite you to tour with them – and pay you next time.

That's exactly what happened to me. I went from paying $500 a night to be on tour to getting paid $500 a night, plus food and hotels.

If you like playing live I do think buying onto a big tour is a much faster way to get your songs out there than slugging it out playing headlining shows to no one.

#3 – Reach out to influencers

You can reach out to different fashion and music influencers who have an online following and pay to have your music posted on their social media. Not only are you buying into this person's fan base, but you're getting a strong referral which could bring in more sales and awareness of your music than a Rolling Stones interview.

I was running a crowd-funding campaign for my one of my albums and one day I suddenly got a ton more sales – that's when I realized my friend with over 50,000 followers on Instagram posted about it like I asked him too. When a real artist or influencer promotes your music, they can have more impact than ads or radio because of the trust they've built with their audience. Now is the time to make a list of bloggers, tastemakers and trendsetters in your genre of music who you can reach out too. If your music is hot and fresh these influencers are always willing to share it with their audience. Just make sure, if you are asking a favor of a fellow artist to post for you, that you're also willing to post for them. We call this a post swap or promo swap.

#4 – Online website advertising

There are a ton of different music blogs and websites for almost every kind of music genre imaginable. Country, Hip Hop, Christian, Rock, Metal, EDM ... and the list goes on. You can pay to have your music featured on these websites as a banner ad. If you're interested in this, look for the button that says 'advertising' and email them with a request to see their Media Kit. A Media Kit has all the pricing and different packages you can buy to promote your music on their site. Some packages will also include email blasts to their list as well as posting on their social media. Personally, I don't promote on websites unless it includes an email blast to the list plus a re-send to the un-opens. Always negotiate down because most websites will offer you a discount or an independent artist's rate.

#5 – Radio ads

At the time of writing this book, most major labels still use radio as their primary method of breaking an artist into the mainstream, especially in the Pop genre. Radio still has that massive ability to make an artist, and record labels are still the gatekeepers to the majority of these stations. This doesn't mean you can't break through as an indie artist, and neither does it mean there aren't other radio formats that you can get played on, like college or smaller independent stations and markets.

I met an artist in a band who had a single in the Top 40 in Canada after he sent the song to station after station, who all added the song. Within a short period of time his band had a massive radio hit and they were selling records like crazy. The power of radio literally blew them up almost overnight, and they got to play some amazing tours off the back of this. But then they started to receive calls from labels who wanted sign them. In fact, even the radio stations told them they were receiving pressure from the labels asking why they kept playing this indie artist's record? The stations buckled under the labels' demands and told the artist that they couldn't keep playing their record *unless* they signed with one of the big three major labels.

I hate to say it, but unfortunately the radio game is rigged against indie artists to a certain level of success . That doesn't mean that you can't take your hit song and leverage better terms on your record deal. It's better to have the labels coming to you with a deal in hand instead of you approaching them.

The most success I ever had at radio was when I was signed to a label, except for a few instances with Active Rock in the USA and Top 40 in Canada.

Radio is addictive – like gambling – because that's what it is: a gamble. It's expensive, risky and it can take a lot of money to make it work. But if you do get a radio hit the pay back is massive in the form of publishing royalties, sales, and touring opportunities.

Beware of traditional PR

I've already shared my bad experience with hiring a promotions team, and I have similar reservations when it comes to seeking traditional PR such as TV spots and magazine features. Ryan Holiday, in his book Perennial Seller, has this to say about traditional PR: "It's like a firework – it looks pretty but ends up being mostly noise and then smoke."

Your goal as an artist isn't to get press just so that you can have bragging rights to your friends and tickle your ego. The purpose of press is to bring awareness to your music, and chiefly – to sell albums and singles.

You might feel important being interviewed or seeing your song on television, but did it sell any albums? You have to be careful you're not chasing vanity just so you can feel good while your music stays in obscurity.

I've been featured in Forbes, Entrepreneur, and performed on major TV networks and yes, the social proof is great, but did it sell any albums? Did anybody see it? I remember getting to brag to friends that I was performing at a big festival … until I found out when my time slot was. I was on minutes after they opened the gates, so barely anyone saw me perform.

I cringe just thinking about the tens of thousands of dollars I've spent for a few articles, reviews and TV interviews with nothing really to show for it. I remember being interviewed in downtown Toronto for MTV and the coolest thing that came from that was meeting Alice Cooper backstage in the green room.

On the other hand, even though your performance on TV or at a festival might not sell a lot of albums, mentioning them in your bio and your website can leverage bigger opportunities. This is exactly what radio promoters do when one station has played your song. They say, "Well, so and so is playing it already, why don't you give it a try?" Then they go to the third station and say, "These two stations have already added the song and are playing it…" These sorts of games go on all the time and are great for impressing the gatekeepers in the music industry.

And so that completes our exploration into the various methods you can use to market your songs. I recommend you play and have fun with them – see the process as an experiment, a journey.

I do truly believe you can keep your integrity while selling your music. What's more honest than putting a piece of your soul out into the world, and doing all you can so that people can connect with it?

I can't wait to connect with your music when you release it. If this book helps you to write and release a song – I'd love to hear about it. Reach me at https://www.smartmusicbusiness.com

Before I sign off, I have a few more words to share with you.

Epilogue:
IT'S TIME TO WRITE YOUR DREAMS

> *"When the record book on you is finished, let it show your wins and losses. But don't let it show you didn't try." – Jim Rohn*

I really hope this book has motivated and inspired you to realize your dreams as a songwriting artist. It's been a blast for me to write it; one of my passions in life is sharing what I've learnt with others so they can bloom and grow as quickly and smoothly as possible.

Do you know you have the power to write your own destiny with your songs?

Now it's time for you to take the first step.

And the next.

And the next.

Here's a question: if your songwriting life is still the same six months from now, would you be okay with that?

HOW TO WRITE AND RELEASE YOUR FIRST SONG

I'm assuming not.

Some days you're going to wake up and not feel like writing.

Some days you're going to doubt yourself and your songs.

I've been there. I still go there from time to time.

A while ago, I had a song demo I wasn't sure about called *Supernatural*.

I almost threw it in the trash on my computer hard drive – but then I played it for my friends and they freaked out about it. That song has gone on to become a fan favorite off my best-selling album *The Chase*.

The message is this: Don't let fear or lack of self-confidence stop you from publishing your songs.

You might get a discouraging email, or comment from a hater.

Don't let that drag you down.

There are fans all over the world waiting to hear your songs.

You have a message that only you can write

When your music touches a stranger and they reach out to tell you ... wow, I have a hard time putting words to what that experience feels like. I only have to look at the comment section under my songs on social media and my spirit soars. I'll share a few of these comments with you, because I want you to know that you have the capacity impact other people in the exact same way. Sometimes it's just people saying they liked a song; other times I know it's meant something special to them.

> "I'm really digging this, the words to the song are some of my everyday thoughts."

> "Wow, how are you in my head? Been in such a dark place. Needed to hear this."

> "This was the perfect song for today. Thanks for sharing."

> "I am really loving this song and I am Linkin Parks oldest fan. I am now your oldest fan."

> "I love this song and I totally downloaded all your songs. Thanks for good music!!! Keep it up."

> "Awesome song ... great lyrics ... keep up the good hard work. Definitely be looking forward to hearing more of your music."

HOW TO WRITE AND RELEASE YOUR FIRST SONG

I hope you know I didn't share those comments to brag, but to inspire you to finish writing and start releasing your songs. I want you to get that kind of feedback too.

Start now. Sometimes inspiration strikes like lighting, and when it does I recommend you ride that sucker as long as you can before it stops.

Other times you have to work for it, dig for it, and finally you strike gold and the ideas start flowing.

Perseverance is key.

Pull something deep from your soul.

Write.

Your words are your weapons.

Your words are your love.

Chris.

www.ingramcontent.com/pod-product-compliance
Lightning Source LLC
Chambersburg PA
CBHW051946290426
44110CB00015B/2136